P9-DDK-946

Be a
Great
Parent

Be a Great Parent

Dr. H. Norman WRIGHT

Bringing Home the Message for Life

COOK COMMUNICATIONS MINISTRIES
Colorado Springs, Colorado • Paris, Ontario
KINGSWAY COMMUNICATIONS LTD
Eastbourne, England

Life Journey® is an imprint of
Cook Communications Ministries, Colorado Springs, CO 80918
Cook Communications, Paris, Ontario
Kingsway Communications, Eastbourne, England

previous ISBN: 0-7814-3688-5

First edition published by Faith Parenting under the title *Pre-Hysteric Parenting* © 2001.

Cover Design: Jeffrey P. Barnes
Cover Photo Credit: ©Rubber Ball Productions

First Printing, 2006
Printed in the United States of America

1 2 3 4 5 6 7 8 9 10 Printing/Year 10 09 08 07 06

ISBN-13: 978-0-7814-4402-6
ISBN-10: 0-7814-4402-0

LCCN: 2006927279

CONTENTS

Secret 1: Great Parents Know They Can't Do It Alone 7

Secret 2: Great Parents Understand the Unique Pressures of Growing Up in America 23

Secret 3: Great Parents Understand the Consequences of Overindulgence 43

Secret 4: Great Parents Give ... but Not Too Much . . 63

Secret 5: Great Parents Challenge Their Kids ... but Not Too Much 83

Secret 6: Great Parents Know How to Avoid Spoiling Their Children 103

Secret 7: Great Parents Work to Be Great Communicators 121

Secret 8: Great Parents Know How to Use the Tools of Listening and Timing 137

Secret 9: Great Parents Pay Attention to a Child's Emotions 155

Secret 10: Great Parents Avoid These Ten Steps to Disaster 173

Secret 11: Great Parents Learn to be Limit-Setters . . . 189

Secret 12: Great Parents Stay Focused on the Final Goal 213

Readers' Guide 223

Notes 247

About the Author 253

1

Secret 1

Great Parents Know They Can't Do It Alone

The first step in being a truly great parent is to admit you simply can't be a great parent—without help from God. That truth is both humbling and freeing, and opens up the door to incorporating sincere, effective prayer into your parenting role.

How are you praying for your child? What *is* the best way for parents to pray for their children? Is there a set way, formula, principle, or guideline to follow? Just how important is praying for your children?

This chapter is a compilation of the thoughts of several praying parents and what they have done through the years. Even before you consider how and what to pray for, remember that the first step is doing what Hannah did. Her story is recorded in 1 Samuel of the Bible. She had been unable to conceive a child, and when she finally did—miraculously—give birth, she gave her child back to God; she relinquished her child into his care. "I prayed for this child," she said, "and the LORD has granted me what I asked of him. So now I give him to the LORD. For his whole life he will be given over to the LORD" (1 Sam. 1:27–28).

LOAN OF A LIFE

A TRUTH THAT WE PARENTS OFTEN FORGET: OUR CHILDREN DON'T REALLY BELONG TO US.

Years ago, a Christian publishing house developed a ministry to help prospective parents. It was called "The Cradle Roll Program." This program provided written materials to assist parents who were preparing for the birth of their children. The title of the material was called "Loan of a Life," and I love that title because it reflects a truth that we parents often forget: Our children don't really belong to us.

Some parents believe they own, or possess, their children. They see a child as something to be molded and formed in their hands. Too often, what they have tried to instill in their children is that the parents' needs, feelings, beliefs, and standards are all that matters in life. It's as though the parents are looking for replicas or clones of themselves. If the parents are successful in this, they've helped their children develop into emotional cripples, unable to separate their own identities from their parents'.

We must understand that children are not our possessions.

We've been entrusted with their care and, in the natural progression of life, they will be relinquished at a given point in time to form their own families. Actually, you will relinquish them in many different ways all through their lives as they progress toward maturity. Understanding ahead of time what this process entails makes it much easier to handle.

To understand what "relinquish" is, we must first understand what God is like and what the essence of his relationship is to us. As he is to us, so must we (as far as possible) be to our children.

God's attitude as a parent combines loving care and instruction with a refusal to force our obedience. He longs to bless us, yet he will not cram blessings down our throats. Our sins and rebellions cause him grief, and in his grief he will do much to draw us back to himself. Yet, if we persist in our wrongdoings he will let us find, by the pain of bitter experience, that it would have been better to obey him.

To relinquish your children does not mean to abandon them, however, but *to give them back to God*, and in so doing to take your own hands off them. It means neither to neglect your responsibilities toward them, nor to relinquish the authority you need to fulfill those responsibilities. It means to release those controls that arise from needless fears or from selfish ambitions.[1]

To relinquish our children is to set them free. The earlier we relinquish them the better. If we unthinkingly view them as objects designed for our pleasure, we may destroy their capacity for freedom. We may also cripple ourselves. Having made our children necessary to our happiness, we can so depend on them that we grow incapable of managing without them.[2]

SEEKING THE PRESENCE OF GOD

One of the best descriptions of great parent praying comes from Stormie Omartian in her book *The Power of a Praying Parent*.

> The Bible says, "Whatever you bind on earth will be bound in heaven, and whatever you loose on earth will be loosed in heaven" (Matt. 18:18). God gives us authority on earth. When we take that authority, God releases power to us from heaven. Because it's God's power and not ours, we become the vessel through which His power flows. When we pray, we bring that power to bear upon everything we are praying about, and we allow the power of God to work through our powerlessness. When we pray, we are humbling ourselves before God and saying, "I need Your presence and Your power, Lord. I can't do this without You." When we don't pray, it's like saying we have no need of anything outside ourselves.
>
> Praying not only affects us, it also reaches out and touches those for whom we pray. When we pray for our children, we are asking God to make His presence a part of their lives and to work powerfully in their behalf. That doesn't mean there will always be an immediate response. Sometimes it can take days, weeks, months, or even years. But our prayers are never lost or meaningless. If we are praying, something is happening, whether we see it or not. The Bible says, "The effective, fervent prayer of a righteous man avails much" (James 5:16 NKJV). All that needs to happen in our lives and the lives of our children cannot happen without the presence and power of God. Prayer invites and ignites both.[3]

Now does this mean you receive everything you pray for? No, of course not. Consider this: Of the 650 prayers in the Bible (not including the book of Psalms), only 450 of them have recorded answers. All prayers are answered, but they are answered according to the wisdom of God. Jesus did say prayers would be answered: "Everyone who asks receives" (Matt. 7:8).

Answers could be yes, no, direct, indirect, immediate, or deferred. Our prayers are responded to by a loving God who knows what's best and reacts accordingly. As Jesus reminds us:

> Which of you, if his son asks for bread, will give him a stone? Or if he asks for a fish, will give him a snake? If you, then, though you are evil, know how to give good gifts to your children, how much more will your Father in heaven give good gifts to those who ask him! (Matt. 7:9–11)

GOD IS NOT CONCERNED ABOUT THE SETTING, BUT ONLY THAT WE PRAY.

HOW TO PRAY EFFECTIVELY

One of the guiding passages of Scripture for the way we're to pray is found in 1 Thessalonians 5:17 (KJV): *"Pray without ceasing."*

What does that mean? It means frequent, brief prayers expressed while we're walking, waiting on hold, driving (with eyes open!), or at any time. God is not concerned about the setting, but only that we pray.

As parents, we need to pray constantly for our children. You want to saturate your child in prayer. What can we pray for? Well, *everything*, but if you want specifics, here are a few:

- Pray for your children to be protected from physical, mental, and emotional harm.
- Pray for God's Holy Spirit to make himself known in the hearts and lives and relationships of your children.

- Pray for your children's spiritual growth, character development, and help with any character defects.
- Pray for their views and attitudes about themselves.
- Pray for their ability to say no to temptation.
- Pray that they will turn away from wrong directions they may be going.
- Pray for their daily difficulties.
- Pray for the friendships they are choosing.
- Pray for them to remember that you love them.

If you want an example of a parent who prayed for his children, look at Job. In the first chapter you discover that after Job's children feasted, Job would have them purified. "Early in the morning he would sacrifice a burnt offering for each of them, thinking, 'Perhaps my children have sinned and cursed God in their hearts'" (v. 5). He was concerned and faithful in bringing them before the Lord.

John Bunyan made a noteworthy comment about prayer many years ago. He said:

> You can do more than pray
> after you have prayed,
> But you cannot do more than pray
> until you have prayed.[4]

Sometimes parents become discouraged when they pray. Their children still have problems, and they think God isn't answering their requests. Consider how the great parents in the following paragraphs responded to similar concerns.

> We parents must allow our concept of prayer to be shaped by scriptural reality, for then we will understand that our prayers are not tools with which to

> manage God. Rather, the opposite is the case, because God uses our prayers to manage us, to bend our will to him and brand our soul with his character. When parents truly pray for their offspring, their prayers bind both their soul and the souls of their children into a mystery that ultimately deepens the life of each.[5]

Often the silence of God is a mute sign of a greater answer. Oswald Chambers explained:

> Some prayers are followed by silence because they are wrong, others because they are bigger than one can understand. It will be a wonderful moment for some of us when we stand before God and find that the prayers we clamored for in early days and imagined were never answered, have been answered in the most amazing way, and that God's silence has been the sign of the answer.[6]

Sometimes parents have asked, "What exactly should we be praying for when we pray for our children?" Here are some items to consider by the authors of *How to Pray for Your Children:*

1. That Jesus Christ be formed in our children (see Gal. 4:19).
2. That our children—the seed of the righteous—will be delivered from the evil one (see Prov. 11:21 KJV; Matt. 6:13).
3. That our children will be taught by the Lord and their peace will be great (see Isa. 54:13).
4. That they will learn to discern good from evil and have a good conscience toward God (see Heb. 5:14; 1 Peter 3:21).
5. That God's laws will be in their minds and on their hearts (see Heb. 8:10).

6. That they will choose companions who are wise—not fools, nor sexually immoral, not drunkards, nor idolaters, nor slanderers, nor swindlers (see Prov. 13:20; 1 Cor. 5:11).
7. That they will remain sexually pure and keep themselves only for their spouses, asking God for his grace to keep such a commitment (see Eph. 5:3, 31–33).
8. That they will honor their parents (see Eph. 6:1–3).[7]

PRAYING THE BIBLE

One of the newer approaches to praying in the past few years is to "pray the Bible" for our children. This is simply using passages of Scripture to formulate prayers, or actually saying the verses back to God and making them your own petitions. This is definitely a biblical pattern, as we see it again and again in the Scriptures.

THERE IS TREMENDOUS VALUE IN PRAYING THE SCRIPTURES, ESPECIALLY IN REGARD TO CHILDREN.

Jesus and his disciples sang the psalms together as part of morning and evening prayers. And when Jesus was experiencing his greatest agony on the cross, Jesus cried out the words of a psalm: "My God, my God, why have you forsaken me?" (Ps. 22:1).

Many other Bible passages are recorded prayers. Some of the best known are the prayers of Moses after the escape through the Red Sea (Ex. 15); Hannah's song at the temple (1 Sam. 2); Jeremiah's lament over

Jerusalem (Lam.); Jonah's plea for grace (Jonah 2); "The Lord's Prayer" (Matt. 6:9–13); Jesus' prayer for his disciples (John 17:6–19); and Paul's prayers for a young church (Eph. 3:14–21).[8]

There is tremendous value in praying the Scriptures, especially in regard to children. It's a way to help us resist becoming stuck in a rut. Perhaps you're different, but there are times when I experience a prayer blockage. Words, ideas, and phrases seem to have taken a vacation from my mind. It's difficult not only to get started but also to keep it flowing. Scripture gives us structure as well as direction in prayer.

Praying Scripture is also a way to remember God's character, promises, past faithfulness, and goodness, which we tend to forget. It's also a memory activator. It helps to bring balance into our own thought life. Jeremiah said, "Yet this I call to mind and therefore I have hope: Because of the LORD's great love we are not consumed, for his compassions never fail" (Lam. 3:21–22).

When we pray the Scriptures, we can pray more directly in God's will. Scripture can be used to evaluate our motives and reveal the direction for our prayers over our children. It also helps us pray with a greater sense of confidence and expectancy. When we focus on God's promises, we have a greater assurance of what he will do. We also learn to trust him for accomplishing what he will do in his own way and time.

When we pray the Scriptures for our children, we grow in our own personal relationship with the Lord. We are reading the love letters God has written to us. Reading these by praying them for our children instills his words within us even more. Finally, praying in this manner opens us more so the Holy Spirit can minister to us.[9]

Quin Sherrer and Ruthanne Garlock provide some helpful suggestions in this regard. They recommend "personalizing"

Scripture verses and replacing pronouns from the original passage with names of your children as you pray. For instance, Psalm 23 could be personalized to ask God to guide your daughter (by name) in the paths of righteousness. "The verse takes on added potency as both an expression of praise to the Lord and a declaration of truth to the enemy," Sherrer and Garlock say.[10]

Kent Hughes, a Bible teacher, and his wife, Barbara, share the concept of taking prayers from the Scripture and modifying them for your own family. Consider this Scripture passage:

> I pray that out of his glorious riches he may strengthen you with power through his Spirit in your inner being, so that Christ may dwell in your hearts through faith. And I pray that you, being rooted and established in love, may have power, together with all the saints, to grasp how wide and long and high and deep is the love of Christ t, and to know this love that surpasses knowledge—that they may be filled to the measure of all the fullness of God. (Eph. 3:16–18)

Now look at this family's adaptation of the same passage. This is an activity you may want to do for your own family:

> Ephesians 3:16–19 for the family. Father, we pray that out of your glorious riches you will strengthen our children with power through your Spirit in their inner beings, so that Christ may dwell in their hearts through faith. And we pray that our children, being rooted and established in love, may have power, together with all the saints, to grasp how wide and long and high and deep is the love of Christ, and to know this love that surpasses knowledge—that they may be filled to the measure of all the fullness of God.[11]

The result is, again, a prayer for your children that both affirms God's desires for your family and asks him to bring about those holy desires in the lives of your children.

Submitting Ourselves in Prayer

When you pray for your children, do you also pray for yourself? Sometimes the changes we pray for in our children don't materialize because we're not seeking some needed changes in our own lives.

What changes need to be made in your life? What do you need to pray about? Sometimes the insight of other parents can help us develop sensitivity to changes we need to make.

Perhaps one of the best ways to pray for ourselves is in the following anonymously written prayer:

> *Dear God,*
>
> *I am powerless and my life is unmanageable without your love and guidance. I come to you today because I believe that you can restore and renew me to meet my needs tomorrow and to help me meet the needs of my children.*
>
> *Since I cannot manage my life or affairs, I have decided to give them to you. I put my life, my will, my thoughts, my desires and ambitions in your hands.*
>
> *I give you each of my children. I know that you will work them out in accordance with your plan. Such as I am, take and use me in your service.*
>
> *Guide and direct my ways and show me what to do for you. I cannot control or change my children, other family members, or friends, so I release them into your care for your loving hands to do with as you will.*
>
> *Just keep me loving and free from judging them. If they need changing, God, you'll have to do it; I can't.*

Just make me willing and ready to be of service to you, to have my shortcomings removed, and to do my best.

I am seeking to know you better, to love you more. I am seeking the knowledge of your will for me and the power to carry it out.[12]

PRAYING FOR OUR CHILDREN IN GOOD TIMES AND BAD

All too often we limit our praying for our children to the times when we have concerns for them or they are in trouble. One of the most frequent questions parents ask is, "How should I pray for my children when they're in trouble?" But the other side of the coin is, "What's the best way to pray for my child when she's doing well and living for the Lord?"

WHAT'S THE BEST WAY TO PRAY FOR MY CHILD WHEN SHE'S DOING WELL AND LIVING FOR THE LORD?

In Colossians 1:2, Paul called the Colossians "faithful brothers in Christ." They were living for the Lord, but Paul saw they still had a need for prayer. If your children are committed to the Lord, keep in mind that Satan, the great deceiver, is not too happy about this. Godly children are still going to face temptations. They can get discouraged and will face greater peer pressure and ridicule than other children. That is because they are nonconformists living in a society that has totally different values. They need the prayer that Paul prayed for the Colossians: "For this reason, since the day we heard about you, we have not stopped praying for you and asking God to fill you with the knowledge of his will through all spiritual wisdom and understanding" (Col. 1:9).

In Jesus' great prayer in which he committed his followers to God's keeping, he prayed:

> I have revealed you to those whom you gave me out of the world. They were yours; you gave them to me and they have obeyed your word.... For I gave them the words you gave me and they accepted them.... I pray for them. I am not praying for the world, but for those you have given me, for they are yours.... Protect them by the power of your name—the name you gave me—so that they may be one as we are one. (John 17:6, 8–9, 11)

If Jesus prayed this way for his spiritual children, then we as parents should pray even more for our believing children that they will be protected by the power of Jesus' name. We can pray, "Dear Lord, I bring my children to you. They have heard the Word of God which I have taught them, and they have believed. Now keep them, protect them by the power of your name, Lord Jesus Christ. Don't let the Evil One steal away the teaching they have received, but rather let it grow in them. Make them mighty men and women of God to your honor and glory."[13]

PRAYING FOR CHARACTER DEVELOPMENT IN OUR CHILDREN

In their wonderful book *Praying the Bible for Your Children*, David and Heather Kopp provide specific examples of how to pray for the character development of children:

> *Dear Lord,*
>
> *I spend all day trying to shape my children's characters, but only work from the outside. I'm*

afraid I may not be getting through, Lord. You hardly look at the outside because You know that the inside is what matters (see 1 Sam. 16:7). How can I teach my children integrity?

I worry sometimes that my kids will grow up having mastered all the right words and actions but not be changed through and through by you. Then they'll fold when the pressure mounts.

Lord, use your Spirit and your Word to penetrate their innermost natures (see Heb. 4:12). Make them whole and healed all through so that the beauty people see on the outside is true of their hearts as well. Only you can accomplish this, Lord.

Save my children and me from deceiving ourselves—and along the way keep making us whole all through by your work of grace (Ps. 119:29).

Amen.[14]

You can pray for immediate, specific concerns as well as specific future issues as well.

One of the concerns of every parent is not only who their son or daughter dates, but also whom they will marry. Many parents become anxious about this—especially when their children's choice of a partner appears to lack wisdom. Some parents begin praying for their son's or daughter's future partner when their children are just infants. This is a wise decision and can bear fruit later on when the time arrives to choose a mate. You may want to be praying about this now. It's not too soon.

You may find that the following prayer serves as a good initial step for you:

Prayer for the Future Spouse of a Daughter or Son

Dear Father God,

Please send your Holy Spirit in search of a good spouse for my daughter (son).

> *I pray that this chosen one may be full of love for you, God, and one who accepts your Son, Jesus, as her (him) Savior.*
>
> *May the spouse of my adult child be strong, good, loving, and prudent. Please give my child the patience to wait for the spouse you have chosen.*
>
> *If she (he) has impatiently gotten close in hurtful or sinful ways to another man or woman, please heal and cleanse her (him) of the wounds and strain of those relationships.*
>
> *Please give (name of adult child) the gifts and virtues she (he) needs to be a good spouse for the one you have chosen.*[15]

Keeping a Personal Prayer Journal

Quin Sherrer and Ruthanne Garlock suggest a unique approach to praying for children—keeping a personal prayer journal. I would recommend that you read their book *How to Pray for Your Children* for more, but let me share with you something that Quin said in that book:

> For nearly 25 years now I've kept personal prayer journals, which I fill with requests, words of praise, reports of answered prayers and specific lessons I'm learning through prayer or Bible reading. Here are some entries from my prayer journal over the years.
>
> Heal Her Broken Heart
>
> Lord, our daughter's heart is broken. Please comfort her. It was her first touch of love, and now he's dumped her for another girl. Her pride is wounded. She feels rejected, worth nothing. Oh, Lord, may she realize how much you love her and we love her. Heal her hurts. Bring other Christian

> friends into her life who can help fill the void left after losing her special friend. Help her get her priorities in order and realize her real purpose in life should be to love and please you. Thank you for your everlasting arms around our daughter—your daughter.
>
> Help Me Be an Encourager
>
> Lord, he's not doing as well in school as I'd like. Help me accept his pace. Though I'd like better grades, keep me from pushing him beyond his capacity. Show me how to encourage him, right where he is.
>
> Accomplish Your Will
>
> Today accomplish your will in my children's lives, Father. Have mercy on them according to your lovingkindness.[16]

With transparency and honesty in these journal entries, Quin Sherrer has given us a beautiful example of how we can bring to bear the power of prayer in a child's life. That leaves us with one last question before we end this chapter:

How will you begin praying for your child today?

2

Secret 2

Great Parents Understand the Unique Pressures of Growing Up in America

I feel like a combination chauffeur, ATM, and traffic controller. Ever since the children came, everything in my life has changed. I knew some of it would, but not this much. My friends even say I'm not the same person. Good grief—why didn't someone warn me my life would be transformed to this extent? I thought a parent just, well you know, added parenting to their life and everything kept on the way it was. (How do you spell 'F-A-T chance'?)

"My work schedule (if you want to call it that!) has never been the same, our love life is hit and miss (and fast!), time with friends is dependent on (1) babysitting money (availability, that is); (2) health of kids (are they throwing up again?); (3) availability of a babysitter. I mean, is it worth the hassle?

"And our cars! Well, when we were at the stage of BK (before kids) we had a snappy little convertible. Not now. Our car choice is totally dependent upon what is needed for the children. We now look at size, shape, safety features (with or without front, side, or ceiling air bags—how about straitjackets?), and gas mileage for all the extra trips.

"What I want is immaterial. I don't have top priority. Every decision has to be made in light of the children, or at least it seems that way.

"I have a friend who's a travel agent. When she described her job to me, I just looked at her and said, 'Hey! That's no different than what I do each day.' I organize trips, schedule times to leave, arrange for transportation, and if I'm not available, I call for reinforcements or send them with someone else. Do you want to hear where we go each week? Piano lessons for two children, soccer practice for three, soccer games for three (one at 9:00, one at 10:00, and the other at 10:00 at another location—Help!), Pioneer Girls for two, Cub Scouts for one, orchestra for one, a tutor for one, and these are just the regular ones. There's always some new trip thrown in such as doctor, shopping, teacher conference, or sign-ups for the next season's athletic event. If they don't have these experiences now, they'll be at a disadvantage when they're teens, won't they?

"And everything costs money. Does it ever! And the kids aren't satisfied with just any tennis shoes. It has to be the brand name—do you think they'd wear a hand-me-down? Perhaps I give them too much. I don't know. I want them to have all the opportunities I missed out on. And I don't want them to feel odd around their friends at school or church—so I give and give. I just wish I had more control over my life. Well, someday … maybe …"

Does all that sound familiar? If not, you're unusual. When we become parents, our lives *do* change. And our children do influence what we do, where we go, and, to some degree, who we are. In America our children face unique pressures growing up in our society—and we as parents face similarly unique pressures in the rearing of children.

But to what degree?

Parenting is a challenge, but it's also a calling. A calling to do what? The frustration of two other parents are seen in these statements:

> One parent said, "There are days when I question whether I've accomplished anything. It seems like I follow one child for a while and then another, either trying to head off a pending disaster or trying to salvage the remnants of the most recent one. Is that what parenting is all about? Is this what I'm supposed to be accomplishing with my life? I feel like a janitor."
>
> Another parent reflected, "Parenting is a lot different than I ever expected. Some days I think I'm more of a chauffeur and other days the enforcer of homework. Then there are the times when I'm a censor for TV programs and the chef of a fast-food diner! I wanted my life to count for something as a parent, but I wonder at times what it is. Have I lost sight of something? Am I putting my time and energy into the right areas or is there something else I should be focusing on?"

What happens to your life and lifestyle when you become a parent? Does it really impact you that much? Could one small infant wield as much power and control as they say?

Once you have a child (or children) you will be changed into a different person. A child alters the life of a parent again, again, and again. It never seems to stop. As your child reaches each new stage, so will you. Great parenting involves embarking upon a lifetime of transformation.

SEASONS OF PARENTHOOD

Recently I came across a book titled *The 8 Seasons of Parenthood.* It was fascinating yet shocking, insightful yet penetrating, revealing but also very helpful. I wish every prospective parent knew this information ahead of time. The authors showed how each stage of our children's lives puts us into a new stage of our adult lives. And these are inevitable, normal stages brought about by our children. Let's consider these.

The first season is The Celebrity. Do you know what a celebrity is? It's a person who is admired and emulated by others. In parenting terms, it's the person at the center of attention who is given special consideration because of "the baby." You've now entered a select group who is expected to perform in a certain way and everyone is interested in your every move. As a prospective mother, you're just beginning to discover how your life is no longer your own. What is eaten is determined by the baby, as is what side you sleep on, as well as how long you can work. But if you think your life is controlled now by your new arrival, just wait.

The next season begins at baby's birth—it's called The Sponge. What's a sponge? One who constantly depends on someone else for his or her maintenance and nurturing. It's also a state of existence in which you're responsible for absorbing the baby's being as well as soaking up every fluid known to mankind that comes from baby! In this stage, your life is totally controlled by baby whether you have a high maintenance or low maintenance infant. But there's one more description that you will say, "Oh, yes!" to—it's the sense of feeling wrung out and drained of all of your resources because of neglecting your own needs to meet your child's.

As the next season rolls around, the power struggles begin. The issue is "who's in charge" and the season … The Family Manager. A Manager is one who handles, controls, or diverts the household resources, expenditures, and schedules. This person is in charge of what the children can or cannot do, their training and performance, their diet, safety, etc. In this stage, you're the person to whom others look for information, knowledge, and leadership when it comes to matters with the children. You're supposed to be an expert, but you don't feel like an expert, and you're not an expert. After all, who prepares to be a parent? We usually spend more time preparing to get our driver's licenses than learning how to parent. Worse, you have the responsibility, but everyone else wants the privileges. When you have a toddler or preschooler, control and power struggles emerge. One author describes the dilemma so well:

> Being self-controlled when their offspring gets out of control requires Family Managers to morph into patient and empathic negotiators every day, many times a day. Instead of throwing tantrums themselves, parents must learn how to "make deals" with their little ones when they test their every rule or refuse with fiery defiance being told what to do.[1]

The name of the game now is "Let's Make a Deal," and it's definitely not a TV show! This is a critical time when parents either learn to be responsible, loving trainers of their children or slip into patterns of indulging, spoiling, or coddling.

When your children graduate to the elementary years, you graduate as well—to the position of The Travel Agent. Itineraries seem to be a daily topic. In this season you have the power and authority to plan, organize, and direct your children's activities—where they go, what they do, when they do it. You're their guide and liaison. You want your children to be safe, comfortable, and accepted by others. What will interfere with your schedule are the changes and demands that others such as teachers, friends, coaches, and your own children, make upon you. You may want your children to go somewhere and do something they don't want to do, and your children may want you to go somewhere and do something that you don't want to do. How chaotic or smooth this time is may depend more upon your children's demands and wants rather than on their needs.

Part of the power struggle that can emerge now is your child's desire for greater independence and your desire to hold on to the reins. And just to add a little more adventure to your parenting journey, by now you may have one or two other children. Not only are you a Travel Agent, but you could once again be a Sponge and/or a Family Manager. And thus the temptation intensifies to just give in to the children's demands in exchange for a bit of peace and quiet. Indulging seems to be the answer. It may be. But at what cost?

Can it get any worse? Can there be any more pressure in the upcoming season? The name of the next season says it all—The Volcano Dweller. Yes, adolescence with all its hormonal shifts takes root, and as a Volcano Dweller you live on the edge, waiting for adolescent eruptions to occur at any moment (and, unlike hurricanes, there is no warning). You may live in fear of what these eruptions will do to you, the other family members, and society at large. Your other fear may be that you've failed as a parent. You will be challenged in every area of your life. Some parents love it, others hate it, and for those with multiple children this season could last forever (or at least it seems that way).

The season of The Family Remodeler arrives when the house is quiet (at last) and there are blank spaces on your calendar—your child is out of the nest and it's time to remodel the home. In this stage, there are three areas that need refurbishing. They are known as "the three I's"—identity, intimacy, and independence. Your parenting is now limited, but no less frustrating, as your child has become a young adult who may make decisions and choices that are definitely not in line with your preferences. Letting go may be a challenge. If it once was difficult being needed, you may now find it difficult not to be needed. Conversely, if a child has been hindered in becoming a responsible adult, looking to parents for help in all areas (especially financial), being needed too much may be the theme of conflicts.

Next, you hit The Plateau Parent season. Hopefully things have leveled out with your own children since you are entering a time of perhaps having to parent your own parents. Grandchildren may be a part of your life, and now you can watch your own children experience their own seasons of parenting.

The final season of parenting is The Rebounder. You could be in this stage for many years or perhaps for just a short time. A Rebounder is one who bounces back after hitting some obstacle. It's a time of waiting for others to care for you. You wait for an indication that others need you, want you, and see you as special. It's a time when you wait for responses and reaching out from your children and grandchildren; you look for them to include you and care for you. If your children became responsible, compassionate, other-centered adults, your life will be full. This season is a reversal of your life as a parent—your children need you less and less and you need them more and more.[2]

CHOICES IN PARENTING

> BUSYNESS DOESN'T EQUATE WITH HAVING HARMONY IN THE HOME.

Recently a mother and father sat in my office, the exhaustion and frustration evident on their faces and in their postures. Their four children ranged in age from five to ten. They shook their heads and one said:

"This is not the life we wanted. We're both so exhausted at the end of the night we can hardly say good night to each another, let alone be affectionate. We feel like what we're doing is dictated by our kids and other families around us. Enough is enough. The word *no* is going to be used in our home again. We're going to set the guidelines, not anyone else anymore. It doesn't matter what other parents think—or even the church, for that matter.

"Our kids need time to be kids, to exist, to just be! And we need time without consulting the schedule or where to drop off or pick up. We're having a family meeting this week, and each child can pick one outside activity to be involved in. That's all. We're all too busy, too rushed, and too exhausted. I don't think God is calling us to live this way. The world is. I think 'Don't be conformed to this world' can be applied to our family life as well."

This was a bold step. But they're making it work. They've discovered that busyness doesn't equate with having harmony in the home.

During the second half of the last century, something happened in the family. It seems as though the control shifted from the parents to the children. The pendulum swung from parents being the focal point to children as the focal point in the family. Kids were no longer the "seen but not heard" minority that they once were.

Generational Pressures of Growing Up American

Growing up in America has always presented unique opportunities and unique challenges. This has been especially true of the last few generations.

Children growing up in the '50s experienced a different world from the one their parents grew up in. These children knew nothing but the good life. And when you grow up that way, there's no reason not to believe that it's always going to be that way, so that's what they expected. They weren't security minded like the previous generation. They were consumers. Ralph Whitehood Jr., from the University of Massachusetts, described Baby Boomers as "a self-absorbed generation, a generation that defined itself not through sacrifice as their parents had, but through indulgence."[3]

Dr. Laura Schlessinger has also really spelled it out:

> Unfortunately, indulgence is currently in our societal blood—a deadly mutant of identity and selfishness that appeared with the loss of guilt. Actually, guilt wasn't lost. It was accused, tried, convicted, and sentenced to death by a generation who invented a philosophy of total freedom of expression and behavior—without limits and without judgment destructive to both self and society.[4]

It is so easy to get caught up in the values of our culture that favor spending, indulgence, and comparison with what others have. It begins with the baby showers. They've become a sort of competition to gift the expectant parents with the latest in designer fashion for infants. Plain old functionality just isn't good enough any more. Carter's is ho-hum these days, and OshKosh and Disney are just basic. Baby Gap is pretty stylish, but Baby Dior makes a statement. Go to a children's specialty store and look at the price tags on brands like Gymboree, Zoodles, and Mulberry Street. That's what the "with it" moms are really buying—or at least wanting. Many children are better dressed than their parents because parents are willing to spend more on their children than they will spend outfitting themselves.

> NO MATTER HOW MANY PRODUCTS WE PROCURE, WE CAN'T PRODUCE A PERFECT LIFE FOR OUR CHILDREN. BUT WE CAN WORK AT PREPARING THEM TO LIVE THEIR LIVES IN AN IMPERFECT WORLD.

And consider some of the other costs. Does a child really sleep any better in a brand-new, brand-name crib than in a hand-me-down crib used for only a few years? Do babies really need comforters that cost more than the ones on the parents' beds, or would a plain, warm blanket or grandma-made quilt do just as well? So many expectant parents spend far more than they can afford decorating a nursery that will be in use only a few short years—and for a child who will hardly be aware of it.

At some spas an infant can get an "infant massage" or "workout" for $30 to $40. Is this necessary? Could parents do this themselves?

We have all the gadgets we need and then some for our infants. Take your choice of carriers. You'll be told you need different ones for strapping your child on your hip, in your arms, on your back, and in front. Not only that, each comes with almost as many options and styles as you'd find at the local car dealership. Diaper bags come in many styles as well. Anticipating baby's every whim, they come equipped with pockets and pouches for every conceivable toy, bottle, snack, and item of clothing. Heaven forbid any child should have to do without during a trip to the grocery store!

In an effort to keep your child from every discomfort, you can even buy a Popsicle shield to keep his fingers from getting sticky and those expensive outfits clean.

Thinking beyond the baby and toddler years, what about a simple swing set? Better leave out the word *simple.* Many of these sets cost upward of $300 since they need to be "closely attuned to children's social and physical needs." A magazine quoted a mother's response, "As long as we were buying a swing set we thought we'd buy the best one, so we went for the deluxe, 100 percent redwood, gymnastic yuppie model. It looked beautiful in the backyard, but the kids didn't care for it. They preferred the neighbor's $79.95 metal tubing swing set."

And what's being paid for some of the toys and games that children expect? Have you ever kept track of the cost of every item given to your child at Christmas or on a birthday or during the entire year? The total could be a shock!

No matter how many products we procure, we can't produce a perfect life for our children. But we can work at preparing them to live their lives in an imperfect world. And for that they need a personal relationship with Jesus Christ and a thorough understanding and application of the Word of God in their lives.

Back to historical trends, Baby Boomer children (those born between 1946 and 1964) were used to getting their own way, particularly those born in the latter years of the generation. There were so many of them that society catered to them and their needs. Child-rearing principles were changing, especially under the influence of Dr. Spock. Parents were encouraged to back off from strict, disciplined, and structured child-rearing. Instead, they were taught new concepts such as understanding, respect, and emotional nurturing. These are positive qualities. The problem was many parents went too far, and understanding became indulgence. Children of previous generations knew about delaying gratification. This generation did not. One result was that this generation didn't learn to save. It's frightening to see how financially unprepared for retirement Boomers are. In fact, 40 percent of Boomers and 30 percent of those closest to retirement have less than $10,000 in personal savings. What will they do when they can no longer work?[5]

The results of this instantly gratified, child-centered mentality are perhaps best described by one hassled parent:

> Today's minivan moms faithfully grind the gear boxes carting kids to games, practices, church events, and school activities at all hours of every day. All in the name of good parenting, which today is measured by the number of extra activities your kids are in. And the grand prize? Hurried children, spoiled, ungrateful children, overachievers with underdeveloped characters, fragmented families and neighborhoods and, last but not least, failed marriages.[6]

Those words seem a bit strong? Not if you'd sat in my counseling office for the past thirty years or listened to the hundreds of parents in seminars.

"AFFLUENZA"

Raising children in today's America brings with it unique pressures that great parents must understand. We're an affluent society, and compared to other countries and cultures, the amount of money we spend on just one child is tremendous. But with so much money around them, and with the messages sent by TV, peers, and even parents (not to mention extended family), we've ended up creating a generation with a sense of narcissistic entitlement. Leonard Pitts Jr. writes in the *Detroit Free Press:*

> Our children are the children of entitlement. These are the children who were never shamed enough, blamed enough, held accountable, or told "no" enough to understand that the world does not orbit around them nor exist for their immediate gratification.
>
> These are the children of the new age, the one wherein parents worried so much—too much ... about bruising self-esteem. As a result, they fall apart like a house of cards in a hurricane the moment life deals them a hard slap or two.
>
> If we continue to smooth the way; if we continue to protect our children from the consequences of their wrongdoing; if we persist in eliminating judgment and morality as too confining; if we don't teach our children that the earth moves around the sun (not around them), we will continue to make frail, frightened, emotionally and psychologically compromised, morally vacant, dangerous, aimless, self-indulgent, confused, lost children.[7]

MANY CHILDREN HAVE DEVELOPED THE ATTITUDE THAT A COMFORTABLE LIFESTYLE IS OWED TO THEM.

Many children have developed the attitude that a comfortable lifestyle is owed to them. And they do speak up. The expectations are limitless—stylish clothes and the latest hairstyles, not just for the teens or preteens, but for five- to eight-year-olds. It's not enough to have a family entertainment center; children want their own televisions, VCRs, computers, and, above all else, the latest electronic games.

Skateboards, Rollerblades, and tennis shoes must have the right label or the child's world comes crashing down. So, to preserve peace and harmony in the home, to spare our children embarrassment with their peers—and because we can—we give.

A few years ago, all you had to do was turn on the television news or read the want ads to see the ridiculous lengths some parents will go to in order to satisfy their children. "Tickle Me Elmo" was the toy of choice that Christmas. But there was one problem: There were more children than dolls. Some children were going to have to go without. Most parents said, "Not my child!"

News reports that year showed frantic parents driving to distant cities, hounding toy dealers, and rearranging their schedules to be at stores the minute shipments were expected. Newspapers were filled with offers to buy Elmos privately for many times their original price. And all for a doll that now resides in the back of the toy closet.

Adolescence and its peer pressure redefines entitlement even more so. Designer clothes, private phones, cell phones, and pagers are a must. Many adolescents just assume that what they'll get for their sixteenth birthday is a car. And it needs to be the latest model! In addition, they expect their own credit cards. None of these are earned or need to be—many parents feel they should provide all of this for their children.[8]

The *Los Angeles Times* reported the following on May 21, 1999: "Driven by vanity, self-esteem issues, and society's fascination with breasts, teenagers are having implant surgery in increasing numbers ... receiving breast enlargements as graduation gifts from their parents ... 'There is enough affluence in

Southern California that [parents] say you can have both the BMW and the breast implants,' said an anesthesiologist … It's unfortunate, daughters are being encouraged by mothers, who have themselves experienced the surgeon's knife."[9]

Children used to be able to wait and look forward to something. Most have experienced too much too soon, and there's very little to look forward to. In premarital counseling, I have seen many who just automatically expect to start their marriages at a financial level it took their parents thirty years to attain. But the reality is that many who marry will be taking a step down in their standard of living. But this they don't expect, nor are they capable of handling it.

Let's go back to the beginning of the last century for a moment. In the 1918–1919 influenza pandemic, millions of people died. While few are still affected by influenza epidemics today, we're at a higher risk of another epidemic … affluenza. Some of the symptoms include

- desiring to have more, regardless of what we already have;
- striving to be successful without concern for contentment;
- refusing to be satisfied with less than the best;
- refusing to follow the biblical guidelines for living our lives to God's glory.[10]

Many people today value what they don't have more than what they do have. They look at what their friends have and say, "We need that." Some people "need" to buy lots of clothes. Others "need" the latest model car. Still others "must have" the computer with the latest chips and software. And this mind-set is passed on to their children. It comes from an attitude, not the genes. But the truth is that they don't need it—they want it. God's Word has something to say about our need to accumulate things:

- Those who love money will never have enough. How absurd to think that wealth brings true happiness! (Eccl. 5:10 NLT)
- Don't weary yourself trying to get rich. Why waste your time? (Prov. 23:4 NLT)
- But people who long to be rich fall into temptation and are trapped by many foolish and harmful desires that plunge them into ruin and destruction. (1 Tim. 6:9 NLT)
- No one can serve two masters. For you will hate one and love the other, or be devoted to one and despise the other. You cannot serve both God and money. (Luke 16:13 NLT)

Our contact with cultural values alone puts us in danger of catching affluenza and infecting our children. Part of the inoculation comes from taking an honest look at where we are and understanding that accumulating these things does not satisfy.

THE CHANGING FACE OF PARENTING

Fortunately, there are changes rippling through the parenting generation. Many are rethinking what they have done and what they will do.

While traveling on a plane trip, a father of three shared with me what they do when they are buying one of their children a new gift or toy. They say, "Now that this is coming into your life, we'd like you to select three to five things that you have used and now can do without. These will be given to others for them to experience the enjoyment that you have already had. And we'll have more space in your room."

The children have grown up with this concept of sharing, and it's just part of their lifestyle. And when they see their parents following this same pattern, they soon realize that this is their family tradition. This teaches usability rather than accumulation, as well as the value of helping others.

The *Wall Street Journal* published an article entitled "Bratlash! The Race to Raise Unspoiled Kids." The question was raised, "Is it possible in this affluent society to pass on middle-class values—hard work, frugality and sacrifice?" Many parents are playing down or even denying their wealth and deliberately living below their means. They do this because they realize that if, as parents, they indulge themselves, they're teaching a pattern of indulgence to their kids. Today, those who have money worry that it will be the ruin of the next generation. For too long parents have felt that their value as a parent was measured by the weight of their wallet and how much they dispensed from it to their children. That's changing.

Many great parents are learning to respond to their child's statement, "But we can afford it," with "Yes, we can but that isn't how we are choosing to spend our money right now. You could put that on your wish list and begin to develop your plan to earn the money for it."[11]

We now hear of families who are creating "Family Incentive Trusts" in their estate plans rather than automatically dispensing all of their funds to their children. Some parents who want their children to be industrious are creating trusts that match earned income on the part of the child dollar-for-dollar. Some have even tied the incentive into good grades and thrifty habits. Many payouts are based on the age of the children.[12]

It's good that we want to give our children every possible advantage. My parents tried to do that for my brother and me.

But coming from a frugal farming background, what they gave wasn't so much material; it was experiences and preparation for life. What they didn't have they couldn't give, but what they did have they gave.

What about you? What do you have to give that will last? What are you giving now? Every parent leaves a legacy.

A HYPOTHETICAL WILL

The seven of them huddled together talking in hushed tones, the surrounding room reflecting the many experiences of the owner. The sounds died out when a man holding a briefcase entered the room. As he sat in a chair facing the others, all eyes were focused on him—for he was the bearer of either good news or bad news. This distinguished, gray-haired man was the family attorney who had summoned the seven together for the reading of the will.

Those who await the reading of a will are often filled with conflicting emotions. We usually find grief over the loss of the loved one, blended together with guilt or anger over the unfinished aspects of the relationship and hopeful anticipation of what might be revealed in the will. Personal expectations always exist, whether we admit them or not. These seven survivors were no different.

After the usual opening condolences and preliminary statements, the attorney began to read the will, thankfully brief and to the point. The shares for the four children and the three grandchildren were equal. But what was stated in the will was not what anyone expected. No mention was made of tangible or material goods. Their absence left the seven wide-eyed. The words of the will reflected a deep wisdom that would take time to fathom:

> Since I love all of you, I want you to receive the best I have to offer. That won't be found in items or possessions or money. There is really no need for this will to dispense what I have for you, since it has already been given but perhaps not yet received or understood.
>
> I have spent a lifetime of creating and giving to each of you. There is a legacy which each of you has received. It would be clouded and even contaminated by any of my material goods. Hopefully what I have left you over the years in our interactions and experiences will fill your lives more than what I acquired.
>
> I have dispensed all of my material wealth to the poor and homeless in your names. Now you will be free to experience the blessings of that act, as well as discovering what you were given over the years. And when you realize what it is, consider what you will pass on to others.

If you were one of the seven heirs, how might you have responded to this will? I'm sure the reactions would vary. Some would catch the significance of this unique act, others might not. Perhaps what the creator of the will was saying is reflected in these words: "As each of you has received a gift (a particular spiritual talent, a gracious divine endowment), employ it for one another as [befits] good trustees of God's many-sided grace [faithful stewards of the extremely diverse powers and gifts granted to Christians by unmerited favor]" (1 Peter 4:10 AB).

What do you want for your children? Perhaps it is best summed up in this passage which goes so counter to our culture: "A good name is rather to be chosen than great riches, and loving favor rather than silver and gold" (Prov. 22:1 AB).

As a great parent, you must understand the unique pressures of growing up in America—the temptation to give in to "affluenza" and to overindulge. I encourage you to heed this advice: Give your children everything they need—not to be affluent, but to have the courage to be unique.

3

Secret 3

Great Parents Understand the Consequences of Overindulgence

Spoiled—it's not a pleasant word. The very sound of it brings negative images and sensations to mind. Remember when you picked up the milk carton, put it to your mouth, took a big gulp, and just as quickly spit it out all over the room? You forgot to check the date, and it was old—past due—spoiled, and the taste had a bite to it. It was bitter and sour. Not a pretty sight either.

Remember when you were walking in an orchard of fruit trees and you saw the luscious fruit on the tree? You reached up and selected a tasty-looking peach, only to find when your hand curled around it that the backside was not only soft, it was squishy. It had stayed on the tree too long, and now it was past eating. It was overripe to the point of spoiling.

I've seen some open-air meat markets where the sanitary conditions were less than satisfactory. Some of the meat was all right, but the smell of other pieces told you right off that something was wrong. Even if you cooked it you were taking a chance. Spoiled food just isn't healthy. It's not good for you. Nothing spoiled is good, even children.

ONE OF OUR MOST IMPORTANT TASKS AS PARENTS IS TO DEMONSTRATE (NOT TELL) FOR OUR CHILDREN HOW TO MAKE THE MOST OUT OF BOTH SUCCESS AND FAILURE.

And there's another lesson about great parenting to be found in food. One of the desserts that I look forward to is fresh peach pie at a restaurant near our home. But I've learned not to order it until late in the season. There's a good reason for that—the restaurant chain tends to use peaches before they're ripe. And believe me, they don't deliver the taste they're supposed to. They're hard and sour. You've probably also eaten food that's presented to you before its time. You looked forward to the experience, and then you were let down. Unripe food doesn't do what it's supposed to do. It hasn't grown up sufficiently.

It's the same with children. When a child is coddled or spoiled, you end up with an overindulged, underdeveloped person.

A PATTERN OF OVERINDULGENCE

It's true that all children vary; the schedule for maturity is different for each one. But the overindulging pattern that exists in many homes today actually stifles and stunts the development of a child. There's much that a child can master on his own without any help such as crawling and walking, but with many life experiences a child needs guidance, encouragement, instruction, and the opportunity to either succeed or fail.

How do you feel about failure? How do you handle your children's failures? We'd all like to see our children succeed, but life involves both experiences—and maturity requires experiencing both. One of our most important tasks as parents is to demonstrate (not tell) for our children how to make the most out of both success and failure. The famous words of the apostle Paul do apply here, "I have learned to be content" (Phil. 4:11).

An indulged child is protected from failure, as well as from doing without. How can you know if you are raising one? The following traits might be a good indication, if seen on a daily basis. (It's true that there can be other causes for some of these; reading the rest of this chapter and the next will help clarify the issue.)

First, an indulged child will have little tolerance for frustration. Frustration is a part of life. What a person wants is not always what a person gets. Facing frustrating experiences and developing the ability to accept them and go to plan B is a big part of life. What does your child say when something doesn't go his way?

"Things like this always happen to me."

"I never get what I want. Nobody cares about me anyway."

"It's not fair. It's just not fair" (followed by a tantrum).

Or does he respond something like this: "Darn. I'm really disappointed. I really wanted to do that." Then a few seconds later, "Oh well, there's always another time."

When you indulge your children, you protect them from life's experiences, and protecting a child from life creates fragile adolescents and adults. Children need to learn strategies to handle life. If they don't, tantrums and loss of control will be their pattern. Or else they will simply withdraw or give up, hoping a parent will take over. Too often, an indulging parent rises to the bait and capitulates, but these strategies won't work in adulthood.

What can you do instead? Take a look at Billy and his mom.

Eight-year-old Billy had planned to participate in his Scout troop camping weekend. He came down with chicken pox two days before the trip and wasn't able to go camping. He was terribly disappointed and upset. His mother told him, "Billy, I know you feel very bad right now, but I can think of five different ways you can handle this disappointment. One of them just might help. If you want to hear them, let me know."

In about ten minutes Billy called his mother from his bed, inquiring about her suggestions.

"You really want to know?" his mother asked.

Billy grumbled, "Yeah."

"Well," she said, "here they are. Maybe some are all right and maybe some aren't." She shared with him the following:

1. You could throw your clothes out the window to show everyone how upset you are.
2. You could write a letter to God telling him how disappointed you are and then read it to a friend.
3. You could call a few friends and complain to each of them.
4. You could set the timer on the clock and cry for forty minutes until the bell rings.
5. You could tell me how disappointed you feel, and then we could talk about what we can do about it and maybe plan for this activity another time.

As a result of the mother's ingenuity, she had a very productive discussion with her son.

Many children become passive. Parents often feel the best way to express their love for their children is through "showers of blessings." They don't wait for him to ask, but instead, provide him with everything he wants before he makes any request. The result is that the child, instead of making known his needs, becomes very passive, just waiting for things to be provided. But there's another side to this: He also becomes bored and uninterested because too much is provided for him. His parents, expecting him to be satisfied, soon begin to feel threatened because of his lack of interest; so what do they do? They give him even more to satisfy him, and the cycle is perpetuated.

A PASSIVE-DEPENDENT CHILD DEVELOPS INTO AN ADULT WHO EXPECTS OTHERS TO CATER TO HIM.

Stuck in this cycle, the child's growth is stunted; anyone's would be if kept in a passive and despondent state. He develops the attitude that life is just one big Santa Claus ready to provide him with what he needs. Soon he writes off anyone who doesn't cater to him. He becomes frustrated because he does not know how to entertain or provide for himself. "I'm bored" is a favorite phrase.

Real enjoyment is not part of an overindulged child's experience. Rather, he or she tends to concentrate on bad or unsatisfactory experiences. Even though 80 percent of an experience could have been enjoyable, this child focuses upon the unfulfilled 20 percent. Thus he's insatiable. A passive-dependent child develops into an adult who expects others to cater to him. He subconsciously sets up a pattern of incessant demanding that leads to dissatisfaction, greed, and self-centeredness. Even when he attains success, it does not satisfy.

The Task at Hand

Second, an indulged child has difficulty sticking with a task. Anything tedious and time-consuming is intolerable to him or her. These children start something but there's little follow-through—they get distracted by anything that is more interesting. They'll say, "it was boring" or "no fun" or "too hard" or "what's the point?" Sometimes parents just think it's just "their personality" or they're a "dreamer child" or they have ADHD.

It's true that the patterns of ADHD are similar, but the indulged child doesn't follow through because the parent is too permissive and lets the child get away with not finishing. Not only that, but the parents tend to jump in and finish it for them. They feel pressure has to be avoided at all costs. As one mother put it, "Oh, I couldn't stand to have Sara embarrassed by not bringing her share of cookies, so I made them for her, and everything worked out so well." What will Sara do next time? An indulged child may not learn the satisfaction of follow-through and attainment. And he or she can become very adept at making excuses that parents buy into.

Solving Problems

Third, indulged children are not good at solving problems. To function in life you need to be a problem-solver. How do children learn this skill? By facing and learning to solve problems on their own. How? By confronting the problem and learning how to figure it out. They need to learn what works and what doesn't work.

An indulged child gets to adulthood with a deficit. Someone suggested that problem-solving experiences are like a library—every time a child solves a problem, a volume is added to the library. Some children have a very extensive library to draw from. It's like the main branch of the library in a major city. Others are more like a book rack at the supermarket. There are just a few volumes to select from. When a child is protected from learning problem-solving skills, he's sent into adult life as a cripple. He's fragile. Life can be a threat. An indulged child can feel overwhelmed, make impulsive decisions, and always look to others to handle life for him.

A friend of mine shared the following experience that applies to any child:

> Two of my uncles had ranches outside of Great Falls, Montana, and I could easily fill a day exploring the ranch, getting acquainted with the different chickens, pigs, horses, and cattle, climbing on haystacks, or playing "ditchum" with my cousins.
>
> During one of my visits, my uncle asked if I wanted to see the birth of a calf. "Sure!" I said with enthusiasm. He explained that it was very important for someone to be on hand for the birth. Even during the dead of winter, he would check on the cows to be sure to be present during a birth. He said that sometimes the mother can struggle and lose the calf.
>
> When the calf was born, it was wet and wobbly and struggled to get up on its toothpick-thin legs. It made several unsuccessful attempts before I asked, "Aren't you going to help it?"
>
> My uncle looked at me with a smile and replied, "Gary, that would be the worst thing I could do. Those early struggles to stand and breathe on its own are vital to life." He told me that if we tried to help the little calf stand up, it could actually hurt the calf. That didn't make sense to me. But the calf persevered—to get on its feet,

> to struggle to breathe, and to search for the mother's milk. Each struggle provided it with the strength and stamina necessary for survival.

Much like the little calf, a child needs the struggle and effort of failure in order to develop the skills and stamina to become a functioning adult.

TO RISK OR NOT TO RISK

A fourth symptom of an indulged child is a reluctance to take new risks. Often, because they don't persist and are unskilled in solving problems, they end up feeling as though it's useless to try anything because it's unlikely to work out. In a sense, they may be right. An indulged child often wants to try new things, but now the fear of failure has a foothold in his life. Some children even have difficulty leaving home after a lifetime of having parents pick up the slack for them. They have no assurance of being able to function on their own.

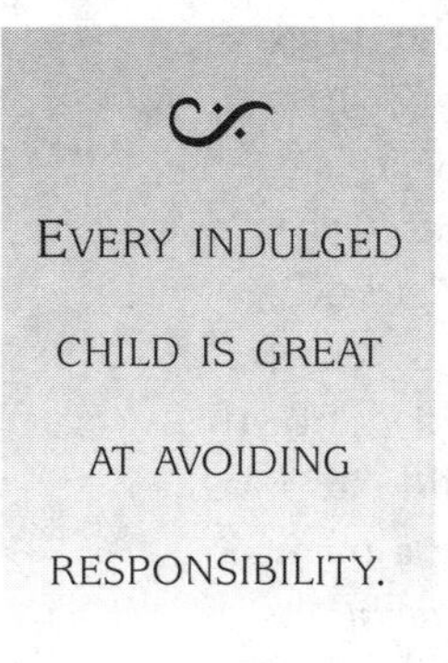

I remember the story of a bank president who announced to one of his younger vice-presidents that he was going to retire and had selected the young man to replace him as president. The vice-president was overwhelmed by both the honor and the responsibility. After recovering from his surprise, he said, "Thank you, sir!" And then, in a very serious tone, he told the old man, "I've always admired your successful leadership. What's the key to being successful?"

The old man paused, put his hand to his chin, and replied, "Making good decisions."

The young man asked, "Where did you learn how to make good decisions?"

With a twinkle in his eye, the president replied, "By making bad ones."

You can't separate success from failure; they're two sides of the same coin. No one learns how to make right decisions without making wrong ones. No one is ever a real success who doesn't learn from failures. And in order to have failures, you have to show up, run the risk, and try.[1]

Have you ever heard the term *avoidance techniques*? Every indulged child is great at avoiding responsibility. They're adept at escaping. "You didn't tell me to bring that in—how was I supposed to know?" Denial is another favorite. "Clean the garage? I didn't know I was supposed to. You never told me."

Indulged children use emotional outbursts to get others to back off. This could include anger, tantrums, or crying. You'll hear, "I'm just too upset to try. Another time, not now."

Some children simply disappear. They may still be there physically, but they stop communicating or interacting. They stay out of your way until it's too late to do anything.

Did you ever fake being sick to get out of something? Almost everyone has, especially in childhood. But for the indulged child, it's often a pattern.

And you can expect these children to cope with life in other unhealthy ways as well. They'll forget (or tell you they forgot) to do things; they may often resort to lying; they are experts at procrastination. The excuses sound justified, but that's all they are—excuses.

Think about it for a moment. If a child is coddled or indulged by a parent—if the parent eliminates frustrations, solves his problems, and bails her out—would this child like to move on in life and launch out independently? Not likely. The kid's got a good thing going. Dependency is a benefit for the child—and probably for the parent as well. Some parents don't want their children to grow up, and then wonder why the child can't function well at church, school, or with friends. I've seen six-year-olds who would go all day with their shoes untied because they were waiting for a parent to tie it when they got home.

An Unexpected Danger

There's another danger to consider. Overindulging another person may be the parent's way of fulfilling his own needs. Some adults have excessive needs to give affection or to "mother" others, which can also include attempting to protect their children from the normal adjustments of life that are necessary for development. Jane, a middle-aged mother, came into my office with her two children. They seemed well behaved but appeared unhappy. After observing Jane's interaction with them, I soon learned why. She told them where to sit, when and how to blow their noses, and when they were thirsty. When I asked them questions, she helped them answer. She also talked about her delight in being able to be such a "good and competent" mother to them.

So when they're adolescents, will they be ready to be independent? Not at all. But they will drive their parents crazy. They will look to their parents to help but won't care for what's offered—yet they won't have an alternative to suggest. Some indulged children stay tied to their parents; some create so much conflict that both parties pull away.

But some teens who don't mature are able to pull away from their parents. They do this by attaching to another teen and becoming overly dependent upon this new person. It could be an overly close friendship or dating relationship, and it's anything but healthy. There's an intense emotional connection that the adolescent wants to be exclusive. Naturally this leads to jealousy and, eventually, the feeling one couldn't survive without the other. The mood of the day is completely dependent on how the relationship is going.

This exclusive relationship continues to stunt this child's growth, just as the parent's indulgence has done. The child doesn't learn how to handle being alone, how to have healthy relationships, how to give and take in a positive way, or how to develop a healthy identity. She may not choose wisely who she attaches to, and the other person may have an unhealthy influence on her.

SELF-ESTEEM

It won't surprise you that one of the other characteristics of an indulged child is low self-esteem. "I don't like me" or "I don't really care for me" will be heard no matter what positive feedback is given by parents. They hear positives from their parents, but in their hearts they know "it just ain't so." Without the ability to believe in oneself and very little expectation of success, fear can take up a crippling residency. Many have a failure orientation. And unfortunately, many will fail again and again.

How does your child handle emotions? Every child is going to be sad, angry, fearful, disappointed, or anxious at times. We were created with these capacities. Part of growing up is learning that these and many other emotions will be companions at times throughout life. As a child grows he or she learns how to identify these feelings, how to express them appropriately, and how to control or postpone the experience. She's not overwhelmed or crippled by what she feels.

But an indulged child is often characterized by the inability to handle his emotions. Very little learning and refinement of emotional expression has occurred. His responses are more characteristic of a preschooler than of an older child or teenager. The emotional intensity or expression is out of proportion to whatever happened. And instead of bouncing back, the child seems stuck.

Have you met adults like this? In many cases the answer can be traced back to a pattern of indulgence. When you treat children as dependent infants, they tend to remain in that state.

We live in a stressful world. For an adult to make it through life he needs to be resistant and resourceful. But take a child who has the following characteristics:

- Low problem-solving skills
- Low self-esteem
- Low belief in an ability to be successful
- Low ability to handle emotions

And what do you have? The recipe for a child who doesn't have much ability to handle stressful events. What most children or adolescents are able to handle, an indulged child cannot. Dr. Archibald Hart talks about indulged children as spoiled children and identifies why this kind of child cannot handle stress:

1. Because spoiled children expect their whims to be satisfied, they never build a tolerance for frustration nor learn to delay gratification. As a result, they are angry a lot of the time.
2. Spoiled children rarely feel fulfilled. Any sense of satisfaction they may enjoy is momentary and comes from the temporary pleasure of getting what they want. But spoiled children aren't able to experience the real satisfaction of

achieving something they've worked for or receiving something they've waited for.

3. Spoiled children become dependent on gifts as tangible proof that they are loved. They never learn the meaning of real love. When life gets hard and they can no longer depend on doting parents to prove their love to them, they discover that a huge void remains unfulfilled.
4. Spoiled children do not live harmoniously with other children. They become selfish, self-centered, and self-indulgent. Consequently, they are disliked and rejected and become very lonely people.
5. Spoiled children are ill prepared to handle stress. Like the tree protected from the wind, spoiled children put down no roots. They stay near the surface and never develop a strong and stable foundation. And when the storms of real life do come, these trees topple easily.
6. The families of spoiled children don't develop real cohesiveness. Children compete with each other to see who can get the most. There is little sharing and much fighting. Family members don't learn how to support each other through troubled times. As we have seen, stress is far more damaging to children when there is no family cohesiveness.
7. Spoiled children live in an "unreal" world. Spoiling parents create a home environment that is far removed from the real world.

WHAT MANY PARENTS DON'T REALIZE IS THAT WHEN THEY GIVE AND GIVE TO THEIR CHILDREN, THEY TEACH THEM TO WANT MORE AND MORE.

> Children who grow up comfortably suffer a rude awakening when they leave home. They find they don't have the maturity to deal with real life problems and consequently suffer significant stress.[2]

Dr. Hart points out another characteristic of indulged children—they don't get along well with others. They have little concern for those around them and what they want. If their actions hurt others, their attitude is "Tough. It's their problem." They end up feeling they're at the center of the universe and deserve to be served. What many parents don't realize is that when they give and give to their children, they teach them to want more and more.

Elizabeth Ellis, in her book, *Raising a Responsible Child*, has a helpful analogy. She says that indulged children live life as though they were in a hotel. In a hotel, you can come and go as you please; someone else cleans the room, makes the bed, etc.; and you can order whatever you want to eat in a restaurant. That's not realistic for a family. Successful family life, friendships, and work relationships require a common ingredient—give and take.

As an infant grows into a preschooler and then an elementary child and then an adolescent, he is on a journey of developing an identity, the ability to say, "This is who I am." Most adolescents can tell you who they are, what they're interested in, what they do well, etc. They can answer personal questions and can tell you what they're for and what they're against, what they believe and what they don't believe. They know what group they belong to as well.

It's not the same with indulged children. They don't have a definite sense of who they are, and they are likely to gravitate toward radicals or misfits as their friends. This feels comfortable, because with them you don't have to be a certain way to belong; you just have to be loyal to the group.

If you ask an indulged child, "What do you want to do when you grow up?" you're unlikely to get much in the way of an answer. He really doesn't know. Goal setting has to come out of other strengths and abilities, but in the indulged child, these are absent. And if the indulged child or adolescent does have a goal, it is either so unrealistic it will never reach maturity, or the teen doesn't have a clue as to how to get there.

Overindulged Children Grow to Be Overindulged Adults

Still another serious risk is posed. Indulging children can damage their faith. Overindulged Christians tend to superimpose their life pattern upon their Christianity. They expect God to be a continual giver of benefits and blessings. As adults, they may look for a church that stresses what God delights in giving to his children; all we have to do is sit back and wait expectantly. They don't care to hear teaching that emphasizes a believer's role in living out the Christian life.

How else could overindulgence affect your child as an adult? Let's look at some common characteristics in relationships:

They will expect others to read their minds. I see a good bit of this in marital counseling. As one wife put it, "Why should I have to tell him what my needs are? We've been married for eleven years, and you would think he would know by now. He should be able to sense what I want!" After all, their parents read their minds. "Read my mind, anticipate, and provide" is the life motto in friendships, at work, and in the marriage of someone who has been indulged all the time.

Life for the overindulged is full of shoulds and oughts directed toward other people: “You ought to know I wanted this.” And when you fail to meet this person’s expectations, he feels that you don’t love him, because that is how his parents showed love to him.

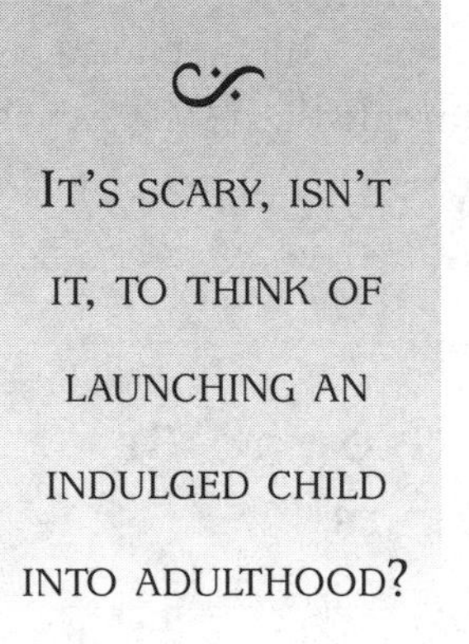

An indulged adult doesn’t make other people feel good, but is more likely to make them feel indebted to him. If they don’t respond in the way he expects, he has numerous ways of making them feel selfish or worthless. An overindulged parent may thank his grown child for visiting him and in the same breath add that the child doesn’t come as often as he or she should.

In marriage, the overindulged person doesn’t listen. A spouse will attempt to make his or her point, but it never seems to penetrate.

If a spouse is constantly dissatisfied, he or she may be overindulged, for such a person doesn’t stay happy very long. Sometimes these people whine when their needs aren’t met, and they frequently lay the blame on their spouses. If they don’t get their way, the threat is always present that they may turn against the one not indulging them.

In his own way, an overindulged person is very demanding, but he often does it passively. He lives with hundreds of hidden expectations, and if other people cannot read his mind, it’s they who are insensitive and unloving.

It’s a setup! It’s a great way to cripple a relationship. If you are married to someone who was indulged as a child, you are very familiar with the land mines: your spouse has placed a multitude of demands upon you, but you aren’t even aware of what they are—and the consequences of not meeting them are great.

There can be other unhealthy behaviors in adulthood for the indulged child. Here are some of the more common forms that overindulgence can take in adulthood:

- Alcoholism. Overindulged people are often bored and lonely, and alcohol is an easy way to dull those feelings.
- Spending. Clothes, shoes, accessories, jewelry ... an overindulged child grows up to overindulge himself. Never having been taught to deny his wants, and not knowing any other way to enjoy life, he makes purchase after purchase of unnecessary items.
- Food. The causes of overeating are too numerous to list, but overindulgence is definitely one of them. In fact, some children who are not overindulged in any other area may have been overindulged in food, and they continue to overindulge themselves as adults.

Well, there's a brief overview. It's scary, isn't it, to think of launching an indulged child into adulthood? It's rough enough out there, even when you do have the abilities to cope with life.

Perhaps you've read this chapter and breathed a sigh of relief to realize that this doesn't describe any of your children. If so, be thankful and keep up the good work. But perhaps the description does ring true. Perhaps you've let indulgence occur out of a misguided sense of love. But before you decide this is what's happening in your home, look at the descriptions again and see if there is a pattern. If so, try to determine what may have brought this about.[3] And take heart—there is hope.

It may not be too late to create a course correction, and we'll discuss more thoroughly how to do so later in the book.

The first step, though, is a hard one—admitting, "Yes, that does describe my child." The next is to figure out, "What do I do now?" Just to whet your appetite, consider these principles:

- Children cannot develop patience or learn to delay gratification if everything comes to them when they want it.
- Children cannot learn to accept their own imperfections if everyone around them is "perfect."
- Children cannot learn to cooperate if everything always goes their way.
- Children cannot learn to be creative if everything is done for them.
- Children cannot learn compassion and respect unless they also feel loss and pain.
- Children cannot learn courage and optimism unless they are faced with adversity.
- Children cannot develop persistence and strength if everything is easy.
- Children cannot learn to self-correct unless they experience difficulty, failure, or mistakes.
- Children cannot feel self-esteem or healthy pride unless they overcome obstacles to achieve something.
- Children cannot develop self-sufficiency unless they experience exclusion or rejection.[4]

God's Word says: "Let us not become weary in doing good, for at the proper time we will reap a harvest if we do not give up" (Gal. 6:9).

Remember Dan Jansen? He's the skater who fell twice in the 1988 Olympics and again in the 1992 Olympics.

When the 1994 Olympics rolled around, everyone thought that this time Jansen would surely win the men's 500-meter race. On Monday, February 14, 300 meters into the race,

Jansen reached down to steady himself in a curve, and the friction of his hand scraping along the ice probably caused the thirty-five hundredths of a second difference between the gold medal and his eighth-place finish. Thirty-five hundredths of a second!

When he stepped onto the Olympic ice again a few days later for the 1,000-meter race, Dan Jansen was 0 for 6 in all his Olympic races. He was feeling out of sorts. He knew his timing was off. He struggled for traction. Seven competitors had already posted better times than Jansen's career best in the event. This wasn't his favorite event, and his prospects didn't look good. But this was going to be his last Olympic race, his last opportunity for a medal. His last chance to prove himself. And to the joy of millions of viewers in the United States, Dan Jansen won the 1,000-meter race in world-record time, ending a decade-long saga of Olympic expectations, failure, and futility. What made him succeed? He had refused to give up.[5]

We want our children to endure and persevere through the trials that will inevitably come their way. And with our guidance, they can.

4

Secret 4

Great Parents Give ... but Not Too Much

John was seventeen and six foot, three inches tall—big and strong, with a gigantic appetite. He came through the door after school, dropped his books on the floor, threw his coat on the table, grabbed some food from the fridge, and flopped on the couch in front of the television. Soon the musicians on MTV were filling the house with their noise (music, to John). His mother came into the room, carrying his books in one hand, coat in the other, on her way to hang up John's freshly ironed clothes, and said, "Hi, honey. How was your day?"

Silence. She stopped and said it again. This time she got an irritated grunt. She saw the chips he was eating and said, "Didn't you find the sandwiches I left for you in the fridge?"

"I don't like turkey and cheese. It's lousy."

"Oh, I'm sorry. I thought you did. Well ... what would you

like special tonight? I can run down to the store and get it. There's still time."

"Don't know. You figure it out!"

"John—I want to get something you like!"

"OK, OK, pizza or tacos."

"Good. John, I noticed some of your pants and shirts are wearing out. Wouldn't you like some new ones?

Silence—"John ..."

"Yeah, I heard you. Whatever." He turned up the volume so all the neighbors could hear what they didn't want to hear. John's mother took his books, coat, and clothes to his room, put them away, and came out. When John saw her, he said, "I need you to type a major paper for me and put some diagrams in. I started it, but I'll never get it done. It's due tomorrow."

She looked at him, sighed, and went to the other room to call a friend and cancel an engagement she'd had for dinner. What she said to her friend was interesting. "Jean, I'm sorry to have to cancel, but John needs me to finish this paper for him. It's overwhelming, and if it's not in tomorrow it will impact his grade. I'm just glad he needs me for something. At least all of my mothering jobs aren't gone. I'll catch you another time. I do hate to miss this, but mothering comes first."

Her explanation is insightful. It appears her feelings of value and worth are tied to her son John needing her. Could it be that even her personal identity is tied up in being a mother? If so, her world exists with John at the center of it. John was blunt, rude, and cold to her, yet she was sacrificing for him. He was taking advantage of her, and she, by doing whatever he wanted, was bailing him out from experiencing the natural consequences of not doing his work. And it certainly didn't contribute to a harmonious home.

And you can bet he will do this again. Why not? If others are there to indulge him, why wouldn't he go for it!

A DIFFERENT SCENE

Recently I talked with a mother at a conference. Of her five boys, four were teenagers and two were driving. (That's a scary thought!) It was a different home atmosphere from John's, though. Before a boy could obtain his driver's license, he had to earn his insurance money. And if there were any accidents or tickets, he had to pay the expenses. These boys were learning that driving is a privilege and a responsibility.

As this mother and I talked further, I shared with her that when our daughter was fifteen-and-a-half we worked out a driving covenant, or contract, with her. We felt that clarifying both privileges and limitations in advance would work better than making it up as we went along, and having it in writing with her signature would induce a greater level of commitment. It did. This mother asked for a copy of it so she could create one of her own for her sons. Here is how it went:

Driving Agreement

1. Before using either car, I will ask either my mom or dad if I can use the car and explain the purpose.
2. If I want to go somewhere for myself, my homework and piano practicing must have been completed thoroughly.
3. During the first six months of driving with my own driver's license, the radio will not be used while driving.
4. During the school year I will be allowed to drive to church on Wednesday nights but cannot take anyone home without prior permission.
5. I will not allow anyone else to use the car under any circumstances.

6. I will be allowed up to thirty-five miles a week and after that must pay for any additional mileage.
7. I will not carry more than five passengers at any time in the Plymouth nor more than three in the Audi.
8. Upon receiving my driver's permit I will be allowed to drive to church and run local errands when either Mom or Dad is along. I will assist in driving for extended periods of time on our long vacations under all types of driving conditions.
9. I will not give rides to hitchhikers under any conditions nor will I accept any ride if I should have any difficulty with the car.
10. I will either wash the car myself or have it done once every three weeks.
11. I will pay half the increase of the insurance costs, and in case of an accident, I will assume half the deductible cost.

CHILDREN ARE CODDLED, NOT JUST BY GIVING AND DOING FOR THEM, BUT BY NOT ASKING THEM TO CONTRIBUTE.

Over half the items on this list were suggested by our daughter. The word *thoroughly* was added to number two by her mom and me. I added number three, which was her least favorite one, but one our daughter said she could live with. The reason for the rule was that too many times a radio is distracting and often played too loudly. Driving is a serious privilege and responsibility, and when one is just learning to be on her own, she needs to give her full attention to what she is doing to perfect her skills. Police officers and insurance agents have agreed with this concept. Rule eight indicates a latitude and freedom for her driving experience. Our family traveled a great deal in the summer, and we wanted her to have the experience of driving under varied highway, traffic, and weather conditions so she would be better equipped when on her own.

Even before this covenant was agreed upon, our daughter had earned half of the increase of the insurance rate by helping paint the family home.

Several years ago I spent some time with a very wealthy family. What they drove, where they lived, and what they wore reflected their wealth. They had two sons. When each boy turned twelve, life changed a bit for each. Up to that time their clothes had been washed and ironed by the family maid. But both parents wanted their sons to be prepared for life, so at twelve each was taught how to wash, iron, and fold his clothes. That became part of their life, and despite the wealth, they weren't given everything. Today they are both responsible adults who realize that life involves work and responsibilities. Spoiled wasn't a word that had any place in that home—and that is a sign of great parenting at work.

Children are coddled, not just by giving and doing for them, but by not asking them to contribute. That doesn't mean a child isn't permitted to be in sports or doesn't take music or art lessons. It means in addition to those things, he or she contributes time and energy to the functioning of the home. Can you list what each child in your family does for the everyday functioning of the home?

Every Hand Can Contribute

I know I grew up in a different generation, but what I experienced could happen today. My main outside activity when in elementary school was music. All sports activities and games were created by the kids. Little League and soccer teams didn't exist. I practiced the piano thirty minutes to an hour every day before school and then in junior high added clarinet practice after school.

I also had what we called chores—taking care of pets, helping to paint our own home and three rentals, setting the table, doing the dishes, and even learning some cooking skills. Now, the cooking didn't always turn out so well! While in Boy Scouts I earned several merit badges, including one for cooking. I'm not sure I really deserved that one. I think the scoutmaster gave it to me so he wouldn't have to eat my cooking again. But still, I was expected to give it a try.

What I remember about home was a balance—I was given to, but I also contributed. I learned everyday skills so I could function on my own.

It's all right to ask children to participate. Every hand can contribute, no matter how small. Even if your kids are tired from school and sports, even if they have three hours of homework, they can still take care of their responsibilities. Don't let guilt or the thought, "It's easier to do it myself," exempt your children from having the opportunity to learn life skills and how to function in a family. Your child has much to give your family. It's your task to discover this and bring it out.[1]

One family had a unique pattern of running the household. The parents and their four children had a monthly family meeting. Part of the time was spent in looking over the household tasks for the next month—things like washing, ironing, cleaning the dog run, feeding pets, dusting, vacuuming, doing the dishes, raking leaves, and washing cars. They discussed who would be doing what, according to capability, what each had done the month before, and each person's schedule. They addressed the fact that sometimes one or another person might become overwhelmed and need someone else's help. And from time to time, they also discussed how the functioning of the family could come to a halt if some tasks weren't completed. In this meeting, they were also reminded to thank others for what they did for them and not to take anyone for granted. There was great flexibility and realism in this approach, and the children clearly saw their role in the smooth running of the household.

> Some parents won't allow their children to fail. That's sad.

I've heard too many parents say, "It won't work"; "It can't be done." The truth is, it can work. Great parenting has been done. And it can happen in your family.

Peace and Harmony

It's easy to give too much in order to have peace and harmony in a household. One mother shared with me, "I never intended for this to happen. I always wanted to be a parent. I had visions of this peaceful home, not like the one I came from. And at times it is peaceful. But lately I've been wondering about the cost. Some days I feel like a giant dispensing machine for the kids. But there's a difference between a real dispensing machine and me. In the others you put in money to get something. There's a trade-off. Me? I see a child walk by or approach me and it's like I start giving. I feel like there's always one child after me for something. No child in our family knows the meaning of the word *no*."

Some parents, though, have been bitten by a bug. It's called the rescue bug. They have the most difficult time watching their children feel hurt, frustrated, or disappointed—so, without even thinking, they rush in to rescue the child and protect him from any of these experiences. It's easy for any parent to fall into this. I know. I've been there. You end up with a struggle between your head and your heart. Each one is sending you a different message. And those who make their decisions with their hearts will have the most difficulties.

Have you ever flown in a helicopter? What's amazing about this machine is that it can climb straight up, hover in one spot, and dart around in different directions like a giant fly. Helicopters have an important job to do. They hover, rescue, and protect.

Some parents are like helicopters, hovering over their children's heads to provide constant protection. Perhaps you've seen them, darting into their children's world with forgotten lunches and coats and homework and sports equipment. They pick up the slack for their children, solving problems wherever they go. They're a self-appointed search-and-rescue team.

Why do they do this? They say it's because they love their children. They can't stand to see them hurt. Perhaps that's because when their children hurt, they hurt as well. Yet these parents may be confused. They think that love, protection, and caring are all the same, but they aren't.

Some parents won't allow their children to fail. That's sad. Failure is one of the greatest learning experiences of life. When you do something wrong, it provides you with the opportunity to do it right the next time. But helicopter parents see their children's failures as their own. They rescue because of their own needs. It's interesting to note in the Bible that God used failure for some of his greatest lessons of life. In fact, all through the Scripture we see him using people who failed.

So in many cases we end up rescuing a child who doesn't

need to be rescued—and who shouldn't be rescued. It's an act of love and sacrifice to rescue a swimmer who is drowning. It's not an act of love and sacrifice to rescue a swimmer who isn't drowning.

Just keep this thought in mind: If we rescue our children from failure now, someday they will really fail and we won't be there. And they won't know how to handle it. Let them learn now so they can be prepared later.[2]

Tarzan Parents

Someone described parenting like being Tarzan swinging on a rope. We go back and forth from not being available enough for our children to doing and giving too much. Back and forth we swing from one tree to another, trying to find some kind of balance in our life. And the result? Guilt, of course.

Some parents give and give because of guilt. There are many causes for guilt becoming the driving force behind our parenting style. I've seen parents who were overly harsh and even verbally abusive with their children become the most giving individuals toward their children. The change is good, of course—but the pain of the guilt is so great that the only medication that eases it is giving in to their children. Others feel guilty for being too busy to spend time with their children, or for being divorced, or for any of a host of other valid reasons. And children learn how to activate those guilt buttons at an early age.

What is your definition of guilt? Have you felt its bite and control in your life? Guilt is that state of mind in which you're trying to repair or fix something you think has gone wrong. You try to make it up to someone you've hurt. Maybe the following sentiment sounds familiar.

> I'm a divorced parent. I didn't want a divorce, but I'm stuck with it. When my husband and I were together we had plenty of money ... or at least enough to pay the bills. Now I've got to work. I know I need to be there more for my children, but to survive I need to work. Ten hours a day I'm gone. One of my boys is angry most of the time—angry over the divorce and me being gone. I feel guilty over the divorce and having to work—so I say yes to them a lot more than I would if life was different—and it's almost like they expect me to say yes. Yes, I guess I do indulge them. But so does he. When he sees them, it's like a trip to Disney World. And the first two days they're home, it's murder.

For many parents, guilt is a constant companion. In a divorce, the noncustodial parent tries to compensate for the lack of time with fun, activities, money, and few restraints. But it doesn't work. It won't replace the personal involvement. The same is true for the working mother, especially if she knows her income isn't truly necessary.

Have you ever experienced any guilt messages going off in your head? You know, the ones that say:

"You're not doing enough for your child."

"You don't want her to miss out, do you?"

"What will other parents think of you if Johnny doesn't get to participate? He'll be the only one. How can you live with that?"

"Poor little guy. He can't understand why I said no. It's breaking his heart."

When both parents are employed outside of the home, it's easy to fall into the guilt trap. Most parents in this situation struggle with two issues—insufficient time and energy.

It's not only at the end of the day but on the weekend as

well. They have to catch up on household projects and they're exhausted from the week's work. Many of them are aware of the fact that they're not giving enough time in their parenting role. I've talked to many who said, "Norm, I know what the problem is. My kids need more of me, not things, not stuff. As it is, we are barely making it with both of us working. How can we give up this job? And I'm up for a promotion as well!"

Many parents today struggle with overwork just to make a basic living, whereas others are on the career path no matter what it takes to get to the top. Their children are left alone too much, and that leads to indulging and catering to the whims of the child. One parent described it quite graphically: "I feel as though I have each leg tied to a different horse and each one wants to ride in a different direction. I'm ripped apart." When you're pulled in two directions, you end up parenting by guilt.

A couple shared their struggle:

> We both work and realize we aren't giving enough time to our two daughters. So when we are home, we make it quality time. We make sure we're there for their every moment and help them with every possible area of their life. We both go to every activity, whether we're both needed or not.

I'm not sure if they were ready for my response or not when I said, "Could it be you're doing too much for them? Do you see any progress in their lives on figuring out problems and solutions on their own? Could it be they'll expect the same intensity of attention from their teachers, coaches, Sunday school teachers? Often they do."

And so the guilt begins. There are several ways to assuage it. We can rationalize, for one. "I can spend more time with them this summer, after all. They're learning to be more independent. That day-care program is good for them. With this money we can do more things together." All the rationalization in the world won't make it so, however.

Or we can buy our way out of guilt. When you can't give enough of something, in this case yourself, you make up for it by giving something else—toys, money, opportunities. But the giving of things to a child can never be an adequate substitute for personal and emotional involvement. Not only that, we're sending a message to our children on what to do in their relationships with others.[3]

> PARENTS WHO BEGIN THE PATTERN OF COMING HOME AND SAYING, "LOOK AT WHAT I BROUGHT YOU," WILL SOON SEE THEIR CHILDREN RESPOND WITH A PATTERN OF THEIR OWN. INSTEAD OF SAYING, "OH, BOY! MOM AND DAD ARE HOME, GREAT!" THEY'LL QUESTION, "WHAT DID YOU BRING ME?"

Another way we respond to guilt is to give in to our children's demands and fail to set limits on misbehavior. After all, we want to avoid conflicts in the brief time we do have together. As this continues, we become less and less able to distinguish between our children's demands as compared to their needs.[4]

INTENSITY PATTERN OF PARENTING

Guilt can create what I call the Intensity Pattern of Parenting (IPOP). It's an overswing response of indulgence on many fronts that comes from lack of time due to career or even social choices. So parents learn to substitute things for time. Walk through the rooms of many children today. They look like an extension of Toys R Us, Ross, Mervyns, Nordstroms, and Gateway Computers rolled into one, often with their own private phone.

Overindulging may even be a way of life for some parents. There are some parents who are so wealthy that it's no problem to give and give and give—or they feel the need to appear that wealthy. They overindulge themselves, their family, and even others as a way of life and also as a way of competing with wealthy—or apparently wealthy—friends.

And there are some parents who are trying to show love by giving. Perhaps they are uncomfortable demonstrating affection or showing love in other ways, and giving seems like the best substitute. There's a problem, though. Parents who begin the pattern of coming home and saying, "Look at what I brought you," will soon see their children respond with a pattern of their own. Instead of saying, "Oh, boy! Mom and Dad are home, great!" they'll question, "What did you bring me?"

The IPOP with its gift-intensiveness is often paired with a style of parenting that has just recently come into being—PBB, or PBCP. Have you figured out what these stand for? "Parenting by Beeper" and "Parenting by Cell Phone." I run into this everywhere—the grocery store, church, the department store, restaurants, even at church. I'll be talking to someone and all of a sudden they'll stop, whip out a cell phone, and say, "Excuse me. My son must need something." I've even seen parents who correspond with their kids at home via e-mail.

Yes, this is handy, I have to admit. But in many cases, it's a handy substitute for actually being together. Parents who do spend time with their children use electronic communication too. And while cell phones and beepers may be good in case of emergency, the constant use of them is teaching children a dangerous thing: that they should be able to talk to either parent—or interrupt either parent—any time they want to.[5]

This availability may feel good to both parent and child, as may other forms of indulgence. But what will happen when the child forms other relationships in adolescence and adulthood? When others give of themselves rather than material things, when they set limits on their time together, will that be acceptable? It's a healthier pattern, but it could be read as rejection by a child who has learned to associate indulgence with love.

TWO-INCOME INDULGENCES

We've talked about some unhealthy ways of alleviating guilt. Now let's talk about a better way—actually doing something to fix the problem. Some parents will be especially bothered by what is said next. And the purpose is not to induce guilt but to consider some facts.

There are many causes for overindulgence, but one of the most common ones in our society occurs when both parents work outside the home. There are households in which two incomes are truly necessary, but it is my belief that there are fewer of those than most people think. *U.S. News* published an article called "Lies Parents Tell Themselves About Why They Work" that debunks some of the myths that keep mothers in the workplace.

Here's the first lie: "We both work because we need the money."

Now admittedly, this is true in the case of the bottom third to half of the work force. But families with bigger incomes are just as likely to have both parents working. Many have redefined the words *need* and *necessity.* Since 1975, the definition of a "good life" has changed dramatically, expanding to include things that used to be included in the definition of wealth. True, college costs are now higher, and many say they are working so that their children will be able to attend. But almost 80 percent attend public institutions, where the costs are usually manageable even if the mother works only during the years when her children actually need tuition money.

And there's something that often goes unconsidered when two incomes are assumed to be necessary: Work-related expenses eat up most of the extra money. As much as two-thirds of a wife's salary (which is usually lower than her husband's) goes for childcare costs, commuting, additional clothes for work, meals out, dry cleaning, and taxes. The net increase in income is often negligible.

Another "lie" mentioned in the *U.S. News* article was this: "It's OK for both of us to work because our child is in a good day care."

Are there many children in day care? In 1990, more than half of this country's infants and toddlers were in the care of someone other than their parents. Most parents, research shows, felt very satisfied with their choice. But a more recent study from four universities discovered the following: 15 percent of the day-care facilities were excellent, 70 percent were barely adequate, and 15 percent were terrible. Physically, the children were safe, but they received little or inconsistent intellectual or emotional support.

Many parents can't leave work to drop in unannounced to observe the day care, and most wouldn't know what to look for if they did. There are parents who overlook problems since they don't want to admit it's not good. Admittedly, it's true that there are some very fine facilities as well as good, small home-care centers. But even there, the care of the best babysitter is not the same as a parent's love and involvement.

One of the main concerns in day care is the emotional and intellectual development of the child. Brain research shows the period from birth to three is critical for future intellectual growth. If a day care has poor quality interaction and stimulation, the language and cognitive skills of two- and three-year-olds can be hindered, as well as their learning potential in future years. High quality day care, on the other hand, can increase their development. That's the good news. But only a few fall in the latter category.[6]

> A CHILD MUST HAVE PLAY IN HIS OR HER LIFE. IT'S THE BASIS FOR CREATIVITY AND FOR BALANCE.

And we know the child's attachment to his main caregiver is the foundation for future emotional development. If there is a weak bond between mother and child, placing the child in day care can lead to numerous negative results.

OVERINDULGENCE IN OVERSCHEDULED LIVES

There's another form of indulging and it's reflected in what another parent said to me: "You may think I'm indulging my daughter with all I do for her, but every bit of time and energy I devote to her is for her own good. I want her to succeed in life. Some parents just let their children do nothing but play, play, play. If Sarah plays there's purpose to it. It's structured and she learns from it. I want her to have a head start on everyone else. So please don't say I'm indulging her. I'm helping her out for the future."

It's admirable for parents to want their children to succeed. But at what price? Some parents become so addicted to their children's potential for success that something else is missing from their children's lives—spontaneous, fun-filled play. Is it always good for a child to be the one who always reads better and faster, does math sooner, and is taking college prep courses at ten? Have you ever run into the parents who carry their children's certificates of attainment around in a folder to show each and every person who doesn't ask to see them? It's not healthy.

When our children's lives are filled with structured activities, we are both giving to them and taking away from them. Some parents are so used to the highly scheduled, intense world of being productive, meeting deadlines, and holding to schedules that they superimpose this lifestyle on their children. "Hurry up" is their pace of life.

In some homes, spontaneous fun has been replaced by the "play date." As one parent said, "The only way I can handle my over-scheduled life is to over-schedule my child's. And if he complains, I just give him what he wants and that works."

A child must have play in his or her life. It's the basis for creativity and for balance. It's real to a child. It's a way of learning about life and expanding imagination, as well as working through problems.

If you hurry through life you lose. In *More to Life Than Having It All*, Bob Welch said:

> Hurrying means losing perspective. When we're so wrapped up in the stuff of life, we're too close to see the big picture. It's like looking closely at the screened photograph: All you see are fuzzy shades of gray. But when you take time to stand back, that tiny dot pattern becomes a picture with distinct blacks and whites. It becomes an image with meaning, a picture with a message. When was the last time you stepped back and surveyed the picture of your life?

> Hurrying means losing touch with those around you. Time is the soil in which relationships grow. Without time, our links to family, friends, and God will wither. Children take patience. Spouses take a listening ear. Friendships take follow-through. God takes our day-to-day attention.
>
> Hurrying means creating hurried children. Too many kids today are growing up without a childhood, forced to program their days as if they were pint-sized executives. We need to slow them down and allow them the innocence of youth, not push them into the adulthood that will come soon enough without our prodding.
>
> Hurrying means overlooking the value of processes. We have shifted from being a process-oriented culture to a results-oriented culture. Strapped for time, we pay a fast-food restaurant to feed our family. We pay a childcare center to nurture our children. Some even pay a store clerk to do their gift shopping.[7]

Sometimes a child just wants to be a child without having to be taken from one activity to another or having to show to other adults what they can accomplish.[8]

Perhaps we need to exit a bit from our children's lives. One author said:

> The problem is that we step in and do not know when to exit. Certainly some children who are floundering need the monitoring and intervention of their parents to stay on track. But I'm talking about our children who could actually be doing much more on their own, if given the chance … and the time. With them, it is time to exit when we find we are doing the work for our children and they just watch, follow, or wait on the sidelines. It is time to exit when we don't wait for our children

> to ask for help but just roll up our sleeves and start working. Better to quietly make yourself available and invite your child to solicit your help. And if your children are only too eager to enlist your help, even if they could do it themselves, why not give them a chance to try it first on their own before you step in? The ultimate goal of parenthood is to enable children to be able to live and function independently, without their parents.[9]

What about your child? Is he or she too busy? Is anyone putting too much on him or her? It may not be you. It could be coaches or teachers. You as parents have the right to say no. You can speak up when teachers give too much work, when coaches call too many practices, when music directors demand too much. We can't put adult demands on children. Sometimes adult demands need to be changed.

Giving too much, rescuing, protecting, hurrying, busyness—these are not the way great parents build a balanced, healthy family. As you read on you'll begin to discover there is a different and better way. Alternatives do exist, and they are available to you.

5

Secret 5

GREAT PARENTS CHALLENGE THEIR KIDS ... BUT NOT TOO MUCH

What was childhood like in previous generations? It was a simple journey to adulthood. Children were much more on their own to figure out how to use their time. They played, made up games, daydreamed, and used their own creativity because they had to entertain themselves. Now, childhood is expected to be a production in its own right. You don't wait until adulthood to perform: It begins as a preschooler. Who are the producers? Parents. Who keeps the scorecard on everything a child does? Parents. Who is experiencing too much pressure? Everyone![1]

There are some parents who are not letting their children have a turn at being children. Whether it's sports, dance, Scouts, or music, many parents today have made their children's activities their whole lives, putting their children's happiness and satisfaction ahead of their own. Not only do they clear their own schedules in order to cater to their children's, but they attempt to ensure that everything goes well in every chosen activity.

Perhaps a noble gesture, but it doesn't allow a child to learn the tough realities of life—not everything works; you don't always win or succeed; you may work hard and still not get what you want. In other words, the children never figure out that life truly isn't fair. We all need to learn to live with inconvenience, frustration, dissatisfaction, pain, and loss. And it's better if children can learn how to deal with these things while we're still around to help them. That's what life is about.

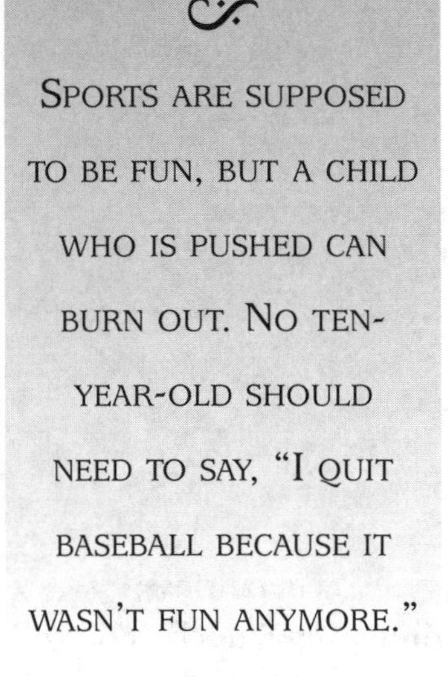

Maybe it's not only our children's feelings we're worried about. Maybe there's a little concern for our own feelings mixed in. I wonder … can you handle the fact that your child may be "just" typical or average? For many this isn't good enough. Some parents do all they can to make their children super achievers.

PUSHING SPORTS

Today so much of children's playtime is structured, guided by a coach. It's true that kids benefit in many ways from playing on teams. They get regular exercise and opportunities for achievement and excellence. They can learn about challenges, patience, and teamwork, and that if you practice you can do better. They can learn to win and lose gracefully, and they gain special skills and coordination. And the bad calls that referees and umpires sometimes make teach them to accept human error and the fact that life isn't fair![2]

Unfortunately, however, sports can also become a source of enormous pressure. If handled improperly, the experience of playing on a team can damage a child's self-confidence as well as his perception of who he is. The pressure may come from inside the child himself or from outside, in the form of parents and coaches.

How many times have you heard parents or coaches on the sidelines yelling at a child again and again, questioning his ability, his desire to win, even whether or not he is trying? This is hard on any child, but if he is a pleaser to begin with, you can imagine the inner turmoil. Add to this the fact that many parents tend to identify themselves with their children's success, or lack of success, on the playing field, and you realize the heavy burden some children are carrying.

A friend of mine has three elementary age boys. One is on an "A" team in Little League, which requires two hours of practice a day, six days a week—plus two games. It overlaps with the soccer season by several weeks, which has a minimum of two practices a week plus games. Add to that the soccer and baseball schedules of both younger boys and the fact that all three boys have to go to everyone's games and practices because they can't be left home by themselves. She prays every day that nobody's team will make it to the playoffs! I love her dearly, but that is one stressed family. And there are many, many families like hers.

Sports are supposed to be fun, but a child who is pushed can burn out. No ten-year-old should need to say, "I quit baseball because it wasn't fun anymore." A great number of kids play sports purely because they enjoy it. But a *Los Angeles Times* article titled "Even Kids' Sports Are No Longer About Play" describes a common scenario. In it, the author recounted a recent soccer match between ten-year-olds. One girl on her way to making a goal was pushed, tripped, and then elbowed to the ground by another little girl who had her own goal in mind—win the game at any cost. The parents from the injured girl's team were furious and yelled at the girls, the referee, and the other parents. But the parents from the other team cheered, shouted, and high-fived the proud father whose daughter had created the infraction.[3]

Just a week earlier, we heard the tragic story of a father who was beaten to death by another father at their sons' hockey practice. Parental violence at their children's sports events is on the increase, as are injuries for children. Part of the reason is the parents encouraging their children to win, whatever it takes.

Why do parents do this? Some parents want their children to excel so they'll have an opportunity for college scholarships. Others want to live through their children, to push their kids to be the super athletes they never were. Whatever the cause, there is an enormous emphasis on excelling and winning. Few parents or coaches teach the children how to handle frustration or defeat. There's little emphasis upon character-building; instead, the teaching is more centered on egotism and aggression. Somewhere along the way, we lost the idea that the value is in the playing rather than in the winning.

So is the solution to swear off children's sports? It's not necessary. A great parent can help a child keep athletics in perspective by being encouraging, but gentle and supportive. Emphasize the value of trying, improving, but having fun along the way.

Be careful, though, not to over-praise. Some parents act like every hit or catch is equivalent to winning the World Series.

And please, avoid saying or acting like your child is the best, whether it's the truth or not. This doesn't help his relationships with others on the team.

Above all, remember whose game it is—your child's. Don't let your child's sport dominate your life.

These next suggestions may be difficult for moms and dads who have a sports background themselves. First, don't analyze the game, especially in front of your child. Bleacher coaches or announcers add little to a child's enjoyment of the game and probably even embarrass her. There are some children whose parents are so over-involved the kids wish they would stay home.

Second, for heaven's sake, don't question the calls! Who are the coaches and referees, after all? They're people just like you—a mom or dad—an amateur. Encourage them. In front of your child, talk positively about them and tell them directly you appreciate their time and effort. It's important for your child to see you model that appreciative, respectful attitude.

PUSHING ACADEMICS

Maybe it's not athletics that interest you; perhaps it's academics. To make sure their child will be at the top of the class academically, parents have new opportunities to push their child to his or her limits. I've talked to parents of preschoolers who have already selected the schools, tutoring programs (if needed), and colleges for their children. There are programs promising that children ages six weeks and up will not only acquire skills, but grow as people.

A 1998 poll in *Newsweek* found that 42 percent of Americans think that children have a "great need" for private tutoring. But what if your child simply isn't academically inclined? What if your child makes "Bs" or just "Cs" in school, even when she is working to the best of her ability? What if your child doesn't want to attend or doesn't make it into college? Are your expectations for your child in line with her abilities? What do you want her to achieve? What do you want her to be—and does it fit with the way she is made?

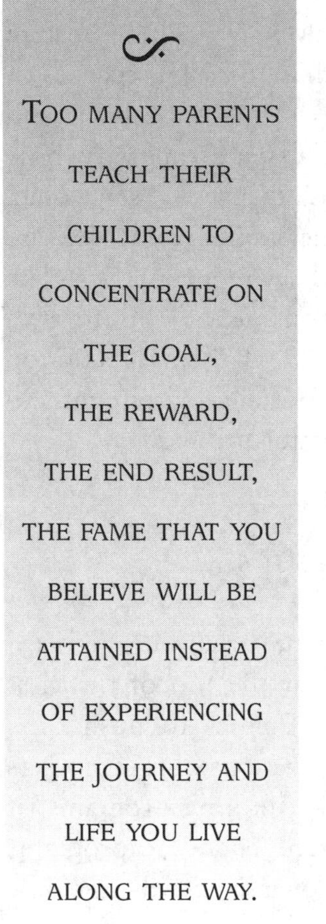

As a parent, I found that I had to adjust my own academic expectations for my children. Since I had nine years of college, I just took it for granted that my children would go on to higher education as well. In fact, one of the benefits of my university teaching position was free tuition for my dependents, and I assumed they would want to use it. But we learned early on that our son, Matthew, was profoundly mentally retarded and would never go to any school. When he died at the age of twenty-two he was only eighteen months old mentally. Surely our daughter, Sheryl, would attend and graduate from college! But after a year, Sheryl decided college wasn't for her. She has always been artistic, so she decided to attend fashion design school. When that didn't feel like a good fit either, she enrolled in manicuring school. Within ten years, she was one of the leading nail artists in the country, winning all of the top nail awards in competition. Now she has her own books published, has nail decals in major stores such as Wal-Mart and Kmart, travels to teach seminars, and recently illustrated one of my books, *The Perfect Catch.* She is satisfied and successful in the field she has chosen, but it's unlikely she would be had I insisted on the direction I had planned for her.

Sheryl has always been a creative dreamer type of child. She would think up things no one else had thought of and create them. This is a dreamer child. (If you're not aware of the characteristics of this child, please read *Strong-willed Child or Dreamer* by Dana Scott Spears and Ron L. Braund.)[4]

Did we have any clue this was the direction she would take, or that she would attain the level of expertise she has? As they say, "We were clueless." She followed her abilities, her desires, her inclination, and her heart, and discovered her God-given giftedness. At times we didn't know the direction it was going or how it would turn out. We didn't need to know. We just needed to give her the freedom to fly. You might be thinking, "But you don't know my child!" My answer is, "You didn't know ours!" Believe me, there were times when we had to fight the urge (compulsion) to jump in, meddle, direct, try to control, or rescue. But we're glad we didn't do those things.

I've met adults who were pushed throughout their childhood, adolescence, and even adulthood. Many have attained their goals but this didn't satisfy. Why? Because the one thing they never learned is that life is a journey, not a destination. If we can't enjoy the journey, it's unlikely we'll take much pleasure in the result. I've discovered that more of my satisfaction is in the process of writing a book rather than in having it published. The discovery and learning process that goes into crafting a book is the source of satisfaction. It's the journey of creation that's important, for I know I will be different after writing each book. It's my ongoing education.

Too many parents teach their children to concentrate on the goal, the reward, the end result, the fame that you believe will be attained instead of experiencing the journey and life you live along the way. And when you get to the goal, there's a sense of disappointment. It rarely gives you what you expected or wanted. And even if it does, the result doesn't last.

Do you ever wonder why people climb Mt. Everest? Is it for the opportunity to stand on the top, barely able to breathe in that thin air, and take in the view? Not really. It's the experience and the challenge. You stand on the top for a few minutes. It takes years of preparation to get there.

PUSHING KIDS IN OTHER WAYS

There's a popular store called Kids R Us. For some parents, that's not a place to shop; it's a way to live! At one of the week-long marriage conferences we conducted for couples, we asked them not to discuss work with anyone for four days, and for one day not to talk about children. It was difficult, to say the least! It's natural to be consumed with interest in your children. But it's also all right to have a life outside the children. For some, that is a foreign concept. I wonder how some parents would handle it if

- you couldn't talk about your children at work;
- you couldn't talk about your children at church;
- you couldn't talk about your children at extended family dinners;
- you couldn't talk about your children in your annual Christmas newsletter.

It's all right to have a life for a while other than the children. In fact, it's healthy—for you, your marriage, and your children! Let them be children. Listen to the words of the authors of *Hyper-Parenting:*

> All for you—even if it means little or nothing for me. Most of us honestly consider raising our children a sacred trust, our life's truest, most important work. We sincerely want to be the best moms and dads the world has ever seen. Yet ... as we've discussed in previous chapters, our contemporary approach has transformed child rearing into one more job to do efficiently and expeditiously, one more performance on which we will be judged, by our children, by other parents, by our own parents—and most severely, by ourselves.
>
> Working to be the best parents we can be, we run and run, and then get up just a little earlier so we can run some more—still feeling guilty that we are not doing just that one more thing. (Assign chores, so as to teach values? Buy a viola, to give the child a special and unique talent? Schedule more quality time?) We are drowning in car pools and suffocating in crowded calendars, trapped by high expectations and ever-escalating standards. We end up ignoring, sometimes even sacrificing, our own interests, friendships, and often even our marriages. We have forgotten or have chosen to ignore our sense of what is sensible. Many of us end up teetering on the edge for a while. Eventually, some of us lose our balance altogether, falling into anxiety, alcohol abuse, despondency, depression, dysfunction, and sometimes even divorce. All because we've lost sight of the fact that everyone in the family, even the grown-ups, is entitled to life.[5]

Pushing our kids shows up in more than just our schedules. Recently I saw an alarming article on what Baby Boomer parents were teaching kids. The author was quite alarmed at what she was seeing. At a housewarming party, she saw a mother giving cups of vodka to twelve-year-old children. When confronted about this the mother replied, "It's only a little. It's not going to hurt them, so what's the big deal anyway?" She also heard an eleven-year-old cut loose with a string of profane words. Her mother's response was, "Don't talk that way in public." Around the house, though, it's apparently all right.

THE STANDARDS OF OUR CHILDREN BEGIN WITH THE STANDARDS THEY SEE IN US.

Another mother takes her daughter and friends, ages nine through eleven, to see a PG-13 movie. She laughs but cringes at the off-color jokes and four-letter words. She questions her own reaction, wondering, "If the theater is full of children, can this really be that bad?" The answer came from her own daughter who said, "Mother, that movie was inappropriate. I didn't think you'd watch something with so many bad words."

I wonder how many children wonder why their parents let them do what they do. How many children have felt uncomfortable, pressured, and embarrassed by what their parents have allowed them to see or do? Romans 12 exhorts us "Do not be conformed to this world" (v. 2 NKJV). Nonconformity to the world is part of our calling to live the Christian life. As people striving to be great parents, we need to think through how that applies in situations like these.

What if Christian parents said no for both themselves and their children to all films rated R? Is our standard high enough? Perhaps even some PG-13 and PG films should not be viewed by our families. What if we asked the video stores to carry other edited versions of popular films, the ones that are shown on TV and the airlines? What if we as parents exercised censorship (which is a good word, not a bad one) of the Internet, music CDs, books and magazines, and TV with its newfound liberties? Shouldn't we examine the words and messages our kids want before they can bring them home?

The standards of our children begin with the standards they see in us. And it begins with us parents. If we aren't comfortable watching something with our children maybe we shouldn't be watching it. It all goes back to example, doesn't it?

Dr. David Blankenhorn, director of the research group of the Institute for American Values, has said that Baby Boomers are giving and sacrificing for their children in so many ways, but at the same time they are short-changing them. If we want our children to have certain values, we have to impart them. We don't want to tell our children what to do, so we don't. Don't blame the music, the trashy movies, or the violent video games. It's time to look in the mirror and ask, "Who's in charge here?"

Are parents leaders or followers? Are parents guiding or giving up? Are parents causing their own children to choose on their own which road to stumble down? Sure, your children may ask, but all you have to do is say no. We're supposed to know best! And most of the time we do, especially when we're willing to be different and live according to Scripture.[6]

If your child is old enough to talk, you have already heard his seemingly three favorite words, "That's not fair." As his desire for independence increases, and as he identifies more and more with his peers, you'll hear this with increasing frequency. The temptation for every parent is to prove him wrong—to somehow justify and "make fair" every situation or circumstance. But the truer thing to do is to answer, "You're right. Family life isn't always fair. Someone has to be in charge and make decisions. And at this time in your life, it's us—Mom and Dad."

THE "WHEN" QUESTION

One day a couple stopped me after a seminar to ask me a question. I'm not sure I was ready for their question, and I know they weren't ready for my answer. They asked, "We want to make sure our four-year-old son does well in school. We want to make sure that he develops his intelligence to its potential, and we want him to read. It's not too early to get him reading, is it? Would we be pushing him?"

I responded with, "Do you want the short answer or the long one?"

They said to give them as much information as possible.

I answered, "All right, you asked for it. Let's consider the brain differences in boys and girls. Let's assume you have X-ray glasses that allow you to see into children's brains. As you look inside you may see a discrepancy between boys and girls.

"In the brain there is a section that connects the left and right hemispheres. It's a bundle of nerves, and there are up to 40 percent more of these bundles in girls than in boys. This means that women are able to use both sides of the brain at the same time, whereas men have to switch from one side of the brain to the other, depending upon what they need at the time. Women can enjoy more cross talk between both sides of the brain. In other words, women use their brains holistically.

"This extra connective tissue in girls is a reason why they develop language skills earlier than boys and will use many more words than the young males of our species. Do you know why boys read more poorly than girls? It's the brain again. The brain that will read better is the brain that can use both sides of the brain at once."

Their response was, "That's amazing! Where can we read more about this male-female stuff?" I suggested the resource, *Communication: Key to Your Marriage*, Regal Books.[7]

I went on to say, "Some boys may not really be ready to read until they are six or seven. If they are made to start earlier than this, they will feel pushed, and reading will not provide the enjoyment for them that it will later on. When you start them, though, it should be enjoyable. But there's one other factor about reading. Does your son see you, his father, sitting down and reading books?"

He paused for several seconds and said, "Well, not really."

I said, "Your example will do more than anything, especially if you turn the TV off and sit and read, and if you take your son to the library each week to discover the joys of books. My own father had only an eighth-grade education and drove a dry cleaning delivery truck for a living. But every other week he went to the library and checked out several novels. He read every evening. I had a great model of reading presented to me. You might want to think about that for your life."

They went on to the next question, "But how can we help our son develop his intelligence?"

I replied, "Well, which type of intelligence do you want to work on? There are several types. There are verbal skills, visual aptitude, athletic or mechanical skills, musical talents, self-motivation, and social skills. And the last two are the basis for emotional intelligence. You see, there are different ways to be smart. Most parents think intellect is where it's at. They want to see a high IQ score, top SAT scores, all As, etc. I've taught graduate school for over thirty-five years. I've seen brilliant and average students. I've seen those that had to have the highest grade on every exam to please Mom or Dad. I've seen those with all As graduate but never make it in the world. There was no balance in their lives. They couldn't function on their own or get along with others. So, have you discussed which area of intelligence your child leans toward and which ones you really want to focus on for him?"[8]

They hadn't considered this, and many parents haven't. I wonder what would happen if every mom and dad read the book *How Your Child Learns and Succeeds* (Galahad Books) by Cynthia Ulrich Tobias while their children were in preschool.

We would have more relaxed parents and children as well as more children who would enjoy school and would reach their potential without being pushed.

THE EMPATHIC ENVELOPE

Consider this: Dr. Ron Taffel, who wrote the monthly column "The Confident Parent" for *McCall's* magazine, said the most successful parents he has met over the years have one thing in common—they all work at providing for their children what he calls an "empathic envelope." His concept of an envelope is quite interesting. It's like a container around everyone in the family, providing a boundary between all of you and the surrounding culture. And you, the parents, are in charge of this container (at least in theory).[9]

It's made up of your values and expectations and your own ways of being with your child. It is helpful if the envelope is palpable. You can feel it expand and contract based on several factors: the age of your child, your child's temperament, the emotional environment in the house, and how exhausted you are having to deal with the above.

This empathic envelope is based on three basic qualities. They're called the three Cs—compassion, consequences, and communication.

Compassion is learning to understand your child's experience as he goes through different ages. It's getting inside his skin and trying to figure out what he needs and is really trying to say to you.

Consequences are your tools for teaching your child about appropriate behavior.

And the third, Communication, is the context in which compassion and consequences happen. It involves adequate time between you and your child for these basic qualities to occur.

It sometimes takes a juggler to keep all these in balance. Your child and you will bump up against each other because of your child's push to grow up and yours to exert influence and be the caretaker. This is inevitable and healthy. Your child needs to experience feeling the boundaries of this envelope. If the envelope opens up too soon, your child won't feel comfortable or safe. Sometimes your child pushes the envelope to get contact and connection, not just independence. If you loosen up the envelope too soon your child will push until you close it again. And if you don't, he'll drift until he finds a place where he can once again feel the security of being contained. When a child acts in a mature way and shows he's responsible, then it's time for you to loosen the envelope a little. When he acts in an immature way, you tighten it.[10]

YOUR CHILD AND YOU WILL BUMP UP AGAINST EACH OTHER BECAUSE OF YOUR CHILD'S PUSH TO GROW UP AND YOURS TO EXERT INFLUENCE AND BE THE CARETAKER. THIS IS INEVITABLE AND HEALTHY.

In order for this empathic envelope to work, each parent needs to recognize the three different roles of parenting listed here and have the flexibility to move through them:

When your child is five to nine you will be The Parent Protector. Your child needs you to help him with his anxieties and fears, explain what he finds confusing and help him connect with the world. At this age he does need supervision as well as teaching and protection. A parent helps him maintain his stability.

When your child is a preteen, nine to twelve, you are The Parent Chum. Your child is in transition, pushing and straining at the envelope for independence and then connecting like a preschooler. Now you need to share her life and do more with her while at the same time enforcing rules and guiding her.

From twelve to sixteen, you're The Parent Realist. You have to be a presence in his life while keeping a realistic view of your adolescent's life, struggles, and temptations. You really need to know who you are and what you value at this time in order to successfully survive your child's questioning.

Now just imagine that you have a six-, ten-, and fourteen-year-old at the same time. You're wearing all three hats and having to figure out which one to wear with each child.

There are two words that we need to be aware of as parents. One is *compulsion.* It's as though some parents feel driven to be involved in every minute detail of their child's life. It's often done under the guise of guidance or supervision. Even as their child gets older, they still try to control every variable of his or her life.

I heard the story of a mother and her eight-year-old son. Around eight o'clock at night, a half hour before his bedtime, he finally informed his mother he had to build a log cabin for school the next day. So his mother said she would help him and stayed up until eleven o'clock working on it. The walls leaned a bit, but it was finished on time. Even while she was rescuing her son (this was her pattern since she wanted him to be successful), she complained about his irresponsibility. Without knowing it this mother taught her son several lessons. Do you know what they were?

- Others will rescue you from your choices.
- It's best to let others save you and do your work for you.

- Even an authority will bend the rules (bedtime) to make sure you succeed.
- You'll fail without help from others.
- Doing it yourself won't be good enough.
- Waiting until the last moment works.[11]

Rescuers are often parents who live with a compulsion to make sure their children succeed.

Another mother who was a successful New York attorney fell into the compulsive rescuer trap. She never scheduled any activities for herself on weeknights for one simple reason: Her three sons, who ranged from sixth to eleventh grade, needed her (those are her words) to help them get their homework done each night. They couldn't seem to do it (to her standards) unless she was there to help. Ever since the eleventh-grader (sixteen-year-old) was in kindergarten, she had sat next to him as he began his homework, and she had continued the pattern with all three.

Hasn't it occurred to her to wonder who will sit next to them in college!? This mother is not living a normal life. Her sons are not learning to be functional children, nor will they become functional adults in the future.[12]

The second word every parent needs to be aware of is *practice.* If your child is going to be able to live life without you and function independently some day, she needs practice—the more the better. It's true she'll make some bad decisions, miss deadlines, get a low grade on a paper, lose privileges, have a toy stolen, eat what gives her a stomachache, but how else will she learn? I know it's hard not to jump in and rescue. I've felt actual pain from choices and experiences my daughter has endured from time to time, and I've had to fight the compulsion—yes, even me—to fix it. But if I had robbed her of the very practical practice of living, what would she have learned?[13]

ARCHITECT PARENTS

Have you ever seen an architect at work? He goes to the drawing board and, in very intricate detail, designs the end product, whether it be a new home or a shopping mall. Many parents today are like architects. Architect-parents mentally design all aspects of their children's lives, including the end product. They believe they are totally responsible for how their children's lives turn out. They have a very clear and definite picture of what they want their children to become. They carefully guide and control their children's activities, choices, and relationships. They screen what they are exposed to and make sure they play and socialize with the "right" children. The words *ought* and *should* are frequently heard in this kind of family.

> OUR ROLE AS PARENTS IS TO COOPERATE WITH, NOT TO SUPERSEDE, GOD'S PLAN AND DESIGN FOR OUR CHILDREN'S LIVES.

We all have a tendency to want to mold our children to match the design we have for their lives. If their unique tendencies threaten us, we try to make these differences disappear. Basically, we are comfortable with others who are like us. Thus, we unwittingly attempt to fashion our children into a revised edition of ourselves. We want them to be created in our image. But that puts us in conflict with God, who wants them to be created in his image.

It is very easy to abuse our parental authority by compelling our children to deny their individuality and conform to behaviors that violate their identity. As parents, one of our great challenges and delights is to honor our children's uniqueness and accept what cannot be changed in them. We are called to guide them, not remake them. Appreciating their uniqueness can greatly reduce our frustration and our tendency to verbally abuse them.

Even when the children are grown up, the architect-parents' expectations are still operating. This may include selecting the children's vocations and the type of person they will marry. If the parents are successful in achieving their goals, they will probably end up with a highly dependent adult child who is riddled with guilt at every turn and spiritually indecisive and weak, with a distorted perspective of God. The attainment of parental blueprints can carry a high cost, not only for the children, but for the parents as well. These are the parents who often experience the big three: burnout, frustration, and anger.

Unfortunately, the key word for the communication style of the architect-parent is *dictate*. These parents often establish themselves as dictators in their children's lives. Parental communication is almost always a directive of some kind: where and where not to go, what and what not to do and say, etc.

Our role as parents is to cooperate with, not to supersede, God's plan and design for our children's lives. God is the one who holds the best blueprint for the ultimate goal and purpose for our children. In reality, he is the architect; we must yield to his design.[14]

Challenge our kids to grow up to be responsible Christian adults? Yes.

Push our kids? No. We aren't called to push. We're called to *parent*. And there is a difference.

6

Secret 6

Great Parents Know How to Avoid Spoiling Their Children

I want to make sure my child won't end up being spoiled or indulged. I want a child who can function when he's an adult, so give me a plan with a money-back guarantee!"

What parent wouldn't like some guarantees? Unfortunately, I can't offer you any. No one can. But there are principles to follow that can help. Begin with the understanding, however, that the parental response to the child is absolutely critical.

Children are different, even within the same family. There are variations in personalities that are genetically based, ones that are present when a child is born. Some children are simply more predisposed to wanting to be indulged than others. Some children react more emotionally than others, some are more impulsive than others, some are not as attuned to the consequences of their actions. But those differences don't let us off the hook. There is still a role we can play in preventing our children from becoming spoiled, no matter how they may be wired.

SUREFIRE METHODS FOR SPOILING YOUR CHILD

No, I can't give you a guarantee on how to avoid raising a spoiled child. I can, though, give you surefire methods for how to create an indulged child. Once I do that, you'll be able to draw your own conclusions about how to get the opposite result. Here they are:

- Do not set limits for your child, however realistic, and be sure to eliminate the word *no* from your vocabulary.
- Do not meddle with your child's behavior by assigning clear consequences to certain actions.
- Do not allow your child to assume the responsibility for his own behavior. Teach him how to blame others and make excuses.
- Do not under any circumstances let your child experience the natural negative results for her behavior. Rescue her—bail her out.
- Encourage your child to depend on you for everything. Learn how to step in and take over.
- When your child begins to show signs of independence, respond by appearing sad or anxious. Keep him umbilically connected to you. This works.
- As best you can, give your child immediate gratification in all areas. Remember, your role is to be that of giver.
- Protect your child from the stressful events of life (failure, consequences, delayed gratification, rejection, etc.).

- Always assume the role of problem-solver for your child, no matter what problems she faces.

If the above isn't working, explode verbally, sprinkling in some name-calling. This will create guilt and insecurity in your child.

> There are times when time pressures, exhaustion, guilt, the desire for some peace and harmony for a change, or parental peer pressure kicks in and we succumb to parenting strategies we know aren't best.

I'm sure that most parents would never state that this is the way they want to raise their children. But even with the best intentions, there are times when time pressures, exhaustion, guilt, the desire for some peace and harmony for a change, or parental peer pressure kicks in and we succumb to parenting strategies we know aren't best. As I look back over my own years as a parent, I'm positive I have followed every one of these negative admonitions at one time or another—just ask my daughter! Occasionally slipping into these mistakes doesn't result in an indulged child. But a pattern of adhering to them will.

Many Ways to Spoil a Child

Keep in mind, there are many ways to spoil a child. Giving too much money and too many possessions is just one way. Not disciplining a child for misbehaving is another. Accepting mediocre behavior when he has the ability to do more is another. And if his requests and opinions are what run the house, then he is spoiled. Anyone who is not held accountable for what he does is spoiled.[1]

There are many things we are to do and many we aren't to do with our children. There are many roles we're to play and many we're not to play as parents. It's important that your child or children never lose sight of the fact that you are their parent. A great parent is not simply a playmate. We may play with our children, but we don't become like them.

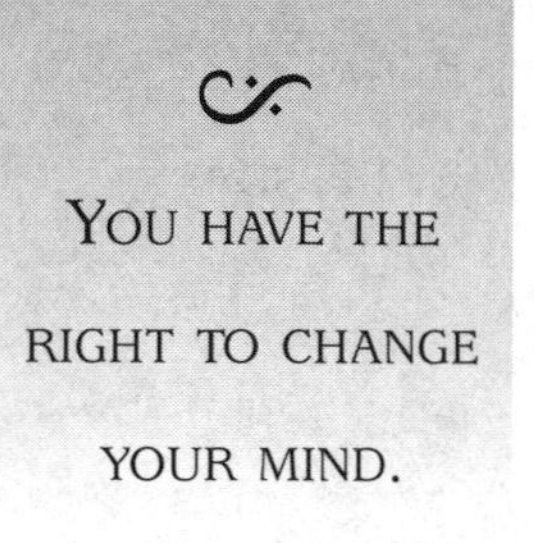

Nor are we to be their servant. A child can learn to manipulate you into doing her work for her. Some parents become servants when they compare what they're asking of their child with what other parents ask and worry a little that they are "asking too much." Once their child complains, "Well, none of my friends have to do that," their suspicions seem verified and it's easy to cave in. But since when did the parent next door become the authority on what kids should be doing around your house?

Children are not equal to their parents. Yet some parents consult with them as though they were.

One author had the following advice for people wanting to be great parents:

> "Children belong on pedals, not pedestals."
>
> "Kids' activities should usually be at the convenience of the parent and not the other way around."
>
> "If you want to create a bored child always arrange an activity when they have nothing to do."
>
> "If you give excessive and unrealistic praise

> to your children you can expect mediocre performances."
>
> "It's better to give them honest feedback than undeserved compliments."[2]

Have you ever considered what rights you have in your interaction with your children? Think about these.

You are under no obligation to make immediate decisions. How many times has your child pressured you to decide about something right now? He comes through the door, out of breath, interrupting you no matter what you're doing, and begins applying the pressure. "Oh, boy, Tom is having a sleepover—this Friday—and all the kids who are anyone are going and there's one spot left and he asked me to go ... and ... and he has to know right now—he wanted me to call as soon as I got home ... so, it's all right, isn't it?"

Pressure—if you don't say yes the world explodes. What right do you have? You have the right to slow things down and not decide at this time. You could say:

"I can't say yes at this moment. You're not giving me enough time. If I have to answer now, it's no."

Perhaps one of the rules that needs to be clarified with your child (posted in writing) is how much time you need for decisions like this.

You also have the right to change your mind; to consult with your spouse; to check with the other parents or the teacher or the coach; to ask your child to present the facts to both you and your spouse at the same time and receive the decision at a later time.[3]

Yes, it's tough being a parent. It's just plain hard work, and you have to be flexible in the multitude of roles you need to play. The more you can flex to the various roles, the greater influence you'll have in the life of your child. As you consider these roles, consider in what ways each of them was helpful to you as you were growing up. Can you also see areas in which these roles might be appropriate for you to act out with your own child right now?

TEACHER-COACH

In this role, you'll be assisting your child in developing some new skill or improving an old one. It is a role in which you will need to give hands-on help at times and at others let your child learn some things on his or her own. Don't think of yourself as a high-powered, intense, yelling football or basketball coach, but think of yourself instead as a birthing coach. You are there to help bring about something that usually happens naturally, but with much greater difficulty.

To be great at the role of coach or teacher, you need to discover what it is your child wants to learn, and when you interact with him, concentrate on what he already knows and what he wants to know. Give your child an opportunity to learn by trial and error. Welcome your child's questions.

LEADER-GUIDE

As a leader-guide, you will help your child explore areas that she can't explore on her own.

On several occasions, I have hired a guide to help me develop my proficiency at bass fishing, as well as to teach me about a new lake. On these occasions, without a guide, I would likely have fumbled around ineffectually and not experienced nearly the degree of success or enjoyment I did with someone more proficient around to help me. But remember, it's important to structure the learning experience in such a way that your child feels comfortable with the amount of risk involved. Be sure to use praise and positive reinforcement as your child moves ahead in any new endeavor. Ask what she has learned and what it means to her.

MENTOR-SAGE

Think of yourself as an actor—but not cast in the lead. When you play the role of mentor-sage you function only as a supporting actor, looking for ways to help your child become aware of what he already knows. Your job is to clarify questions rather than offer answers. You help shed light on issues, but you refrain from instructing. This is, admittedly, difficult!

When we see our children struggling or when they don't seem to be catching on to something important, it's hard not to step in and tell them exactly how to handle things better. It's also hard not to let them see the frustration and irritation we frequently feel in these situations. But telling them what to do and letting them see how we feel about it dampens the child's desire to learn. The rule here is restraint—restraint—restraint! Let your child discover his capabilities. The process may require trial and error, but try not to panic when the errors become apparent.

If your child is a preteen or a teenager, this role is very important. During this time, children test the values they've always held and come face-to-face with conflicting value systems to a heightened degree. It may be frightening to watch, but it's the only way they will ever truly "own" the values you have taught them.

Remember, as you play this role you may hear statements you don't want to hear. Your tendency may be to immediately correct and override in order to make them believe what you want them to believe. Don't! It won't work. Your role is to help your child search out the truth so that it can become his own.

FRIEND-COMPANION

This is a role that slowly evolves as your child grows older. You may see it developing especially during the teen years, though it can begin in childhood to some degree. In this role, you do something with your child that you both enjoy. For Sheryl and me, it's often fishing, something we began when she was five. We have had many enjoyable outings together, and she catches as many fish as I do. In fact, on one trip to Canada she not only caught the largest northern pike of the trip (twenty-two pounds), but the largest caught in that lake all year. Was she ever excited, and was I ever proud of her!

It's important to take time for these opportunities. This is where your playful side has a chance to emerge. Remember that your child may want you to stay in this role longer than you want to or than is best. You will need to work this out.

COUNSELOR-CONFIDANT

At times you will assume this very influential role, that of trusted listener and keeper of secrets. In this role you don't give advice. You merely reflect back what you hear or sense your child is saying. Please, at all costs, don't offer trite remarks when she shares her hurts. Allow her to feel what she feels and encourage her to grieve when necessary.

PROTECTOR-ADVOCATE

This is probably a role that feels very natural—and it's one that's easy to play at the wrong times. In this role, you provide a support system for your child during difficult times in her life. You act out your belief in your child and her intentions. You give her the benefit of the doubt while letting her experience the consequences of her actions. When your child makes a mistake or misjudgment, you don't shield her from the results, but you help her to learn from them and to believe the next time will be different. You do, however, shield your child from hanging on to guilt and from others who won't give her another chance. You focus on intentions rather than just actions. If she misbehaves, you talk with her about what she will do differently the next time.

PROVIDER-SUPPORTER

Parents are the primary providers for all of the basic needs of the child such as food, clothing, shelter, and health care. You would be amazed at the number of families who can afford all this but funnel the funds elsewhere for various reasons.

Besides making sure your child's needs are met, you need to support him in becoming independently able to meet his own needs. This means that over a period of years you are assisting your child not to need you. [4]

OTHER ELEMENTS OF HEALTHY PARENTING

These are the primary roles parents need to play in their children's lives. But there are other elements of healthy parenting as well. We need to be available when our children need us, for instance. Coming home to an empty house day after day can have a very negative effect upon a child. He or she may feel abandoned or get into serious difficulty because of the lack of supervision. Work demands should come second to the necessity of spending adequate time, at appropriate times, with our children.

Parents also need to provide protection from the normal hazards of life, as well as from information and experiences the child is not yet equipped to handle. Media exposure—including television, movies, and recordings—need to be screened, limited, and supervised. Children should neither be pushed into anything that is beyond their capabilities nor prematurely exposed to certain activities and experiences.

A CHILD'S NEEDS AT ANY ONE TIME ARE RELATED TO THE WAYS IN WHICH HE IS VULNERABLE.

It's critical that parents really know their children, staying well acquainted with their developmental level and what's appropriate for them at what age or stage. They need to become informed about what behavior, privileges, and responsibilities are appropriate at each age. They need also to respect the uniqueness of each child and adapt their responses to both the child and the situation.

Proverbs 22:6 exhorts parents to "train up a child in the way he should go [and in keeping with his individual gift or bent], and when he is old he will not depart from it" (AB). This Scripture is advocating respect for the individuality of the child. Wise parents encourage the child to develop his or her special areas of giftedness.

What does a child really need from his parents? A child's needs at any one time are related to the ways in which he is vulnerable.

A young child needs to believe his parents are all knowing and all powerful. Do you think of yourself as omniscient? Probably not. But to give a child security and to make sense of this world he needs to see you this way.

For your child to become responsible, he needs to see parents who function in a responsible, concerned way toward all of the family members.

All children need to receive and witness both physical and verbal expressions of affection and acceptance. Many parents did not receive this themselves and find it difficult to provide it for their children, but this is an obstacle that is crucial to overcome. Children need to be hugged and cooed over, and they especially enjoy seeing their parents giving each other kisses and hugs—particularly after the inevitable arguments of married life. Not only does it reassure them, but also it provides invaluable lessons for how to handle conflicts.

Great parents establish healthy rules and guidelines for their children, but they also teach them how to establish rules for themselves when the parents are not around. At the same time, however, the parents make sure the roles are clear: parents remain parents and children remain children. Each understands and respects his or her position.

Great parents know how to pronounce a little two-letter word, *no*. They understand that this is not a bad word. It is not negative, nor inappropriately restrictive, nor will it do irreparable harm to a child. In a parent's vocabulary, it is a loving term used all too infrequently.

Do you have trouble saying no? Here are some phrases to practice so you can use them easily when the occasion arises. Keep in mind you don't have to justify saying no, nor do you have to explain why. Simply say it calmly, quietly, and firmly.

"No, we won't be doing that right now."

"No, we won't be buying that today."

"No, but perhaps another time. I'll let you know."

"No, this is what we will be doing."

"No, here's the plan for tonight."

Independence, rather than dependence, is fostered in a healthy family. Throughout the parenting role is woven a thread of gradual relinquishment of authority and decision making. This means we accept and encourage the fact that our children are going to grow and change. The child needs us to model this for him or her.

Another important quality of effective parents is the ability to simplify their children's lives. It can happen—it's possible to do without many items. But it begins with the parents' lifestyle.

Children don't have to have it all. I came across some suggestions recently that make sense. Before you say they won't work, try them. You could be pleasantly surprised. And by these suggestions working, I don't mean your children will always like them. Parenting isn't always popular.

You could establish age limits for dating and driving.

How about limiting the child's choices when dining out? The children's menu is there for children. Some families start the privilege of ordering from the adult menu at age twelve.

Have you ever considered limiting the number of toys a child receives at Christmas and for birthdays? Perhaps for each new toy, an old one is given away. Or upon acquiring a new toy, no requests for anything else will be heard for six weeks. What about spacing out Christmas gifts over two or three weeks?

What about clothing? Some families set an age when their children can begin wearing adult-looking clothing or wearing makeup. When you establish rules and standards in advance and have them posted for all to read, it cuts down on hassles. And it's all right for them to say, "These aren't fair." They're not experts on what is fair and what isn't. You set the standards.

You can also learn to negotiate with your child for special

items. If it's an expensive piece of sports equipment, for instance, you might ask, "How much will you pay toward this? Let's figure out your share." And have them either pay their share up front, or pay half up front and the rest in payments.

A friend's son, for instance, wanted an expensive guitar. This was before he knew how to play. The arrangement was that they would rent a guitar, and he would be given lessons. After he had practiced five out of seven days a week, a half hour a day, for three months, the guitar would be his.

Another friend's son wanted a dog and assured his parents he would take all the responsibility for caring for his pet. His parents told him they would like to give him a responsibility first, and if he carried it out faithfully, the dog was his. All he had to do was mow the lawn and sweep up the clippings each week for twenty weeks without having to be reminded to do it. He agreed, but quit after several weeks—and he did not receive the dog.[5]

HEALTHY INDEPENDENCE

In the book *Leading a Child to Independence*, the authors compare the growing independence of a youngster to America's Declaration of Independence. Independence is something that happens "in the course of human events." And since it is so inevitable, we would be better off to prepare for it and foster it. As much as possible, parents need to be in charge of the process rather than be buffeted willy-nilly by the stormy winds of blustering rebellion.

When parents do not let go, the entire family can suffer dire consequences: "It leaves emotionally crippled parents living their lives through emotionally crippled children who then feebly try to perform as adults while avoiding the responsibilities of determining the destiny of their country, offspring, and society. The results are a loss of independence for all—past, present, and future."[6]

Another phrase in the Declaration of Independence is applicable to families with children moving toward adulthood: It states that it becomes necessary "for one people to dissolve the political bonds which have connected them with one another." Sometimes a child decides that it's time to leave home. Sometimes the parent reaches that conclusion first. Each party holds the power to make the decision. And when the implementation is handled properly, the bonds can dissolve in a way that is congenial and healthy.

The Declaration goes on to say that independence is a separate and equal station or position in life. For a while, our country was politically and economically dependent upon England. We needed the security and protection of an established power. But America gradually grew to desire a life of its own. England naturally wanted to protect and keep tabs on this budding colony. Because it was unwilling or unable to let go, the bloody and costly American Revolution had to be waged to sever the bonds. Unfortunately, some families end up suffering casualties in their own smaller version of the revolutionary war in a child's quest for independence![7]

Here is the story of how one set of parents, Paul and Jeannie McKean, helped their children move toward independence.

> As the children got older, we began studying Scripture together....Then we started to talk about their quiet times and the things we were learning in our walks with the Lord. From our journals we shared what the Lord was teaching us. If we had a hard week, we felt free to talk about it and soak up the affirmation of our family. We took our concerns to the Lord in a spirit of oneness.
>
> We also helped Tanya and Todd develop goals

> for their own lives. We felt part of being independent is knowing where you are going. In 1983, we became familiar with Master Planning Associates, which helped us consider questions such as "What are you dreaming of accomplishing five to twenty years from now?" Or "What needs do you feel deeply burdened by and uniquely qualified to meet?" We helped our children assess the milestones they had already passed and the ideas they would like to see become reality. We talked about colleges and careers and our purpose in life. Together we were able to dream dreams, some of which have already come true.
>
> As the children became more independent, Paul and I let them organize some of the family days. Each of the four of us planned one Sunday each month. Todd's favorite activity was cross-country skiing; Tanya enjoyed relaxing at Dana Point Harbor.
>
> One of the most practical things we did during our family times was talk about events to come. Each week we got out the calendar, looked at the commitments, and then planned the rest of the week. When the children were little, they were most interested in free time for play; but little by little their activities began to match ours. Looking at the calendar together has helped us take an active interest in one another's lives and avoid the miscommunications which plague busy families. Therefore we were better able to pray for each other and to understand the pressures and opportunities we shared.[8]

When asked about her parents' approach in helping them grow toward independence, Tanya replied: "My parents have made a lot of decisions for me and yet have made me make a lot of decisions. They have given me freedom when I've shown I can handle it responsibly—and even when I haven't been responsible, just to let me know I'm an individual who has worth and importance. I know now that I am quite intelligent and I can make decisions. Later on I will become responsible in certain areas that I might not be doing well in right now."

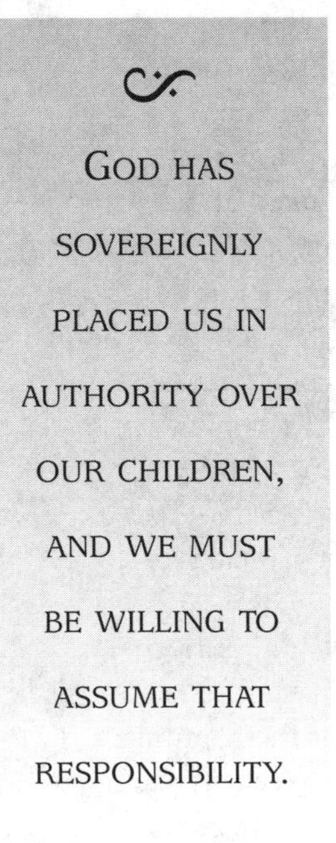

Todd also expressed his appreciation: "As I look back, I know my parents have really cared about our lives and what we've been interested in. They haven't said, 'Kids, we're going to do this because your father and I want to do this,' or anything like that.

"They consulted us about activities we wanted. We spend at least an hour or two doing something with our parents each weekend—different kinds of activities that kids usually do. My dad and I got a little airplane that we put fuel into, and we held it by a string as it flew around in the air. We also got interested in train sets and spent some of our activity time on them. That was really fun! I know most of my friends' parents never took time for special activities with them; so I feel that really shows my parents' interest in my life."[9]

In a letter to his father, Tony Campolo, Bart reflected on how his parents helped him grow:

> That's what real freedom is, I think: the understanding that in a world filled with choices and decisions, under tremendous pressure from other people and our own desires, amid the paralyzing fear of mistakes or failure, loving God and loving his people are the only things that really matter, and doing those things is a decision that we genuinely have the

ability to make in every situation.

You and Mom didn't let me do whatever I wanted to, Dad, but you gave me my freedom nonetheless. I think I finally appreciate it.

Love,

Bart[10]

The Ultimate Goal

The ultimate goal of great parenting is not kids who merely have a knowledge about God. It is kids who have a personal relationship with God. It is kids who really believe that God's Word is relevant for every aspect of their lives. It involves teaching our children the ways of God, helping them understand the character of God, helping them to become sensitive to the darkness of their own hearts and the danger of walking alone and trusting in themselves. It involves teaching them the power of the cross and the provision of God's promises.

God has called us to lead, guide, nurture, correct, and discipline our children. God has sovereignly placed us in authority over our children, and we must be willing to assume that responsibility.

In Genesis 18:19, God speaks of Abraham when he says, "I have chosen him, so that he will direct his children and his household after him to keep the way of the Lord by doing what is right and just."

In Ephesians 6:4, we are commanded to bring up our children "in the training and instruction of the Lord." Children will be good decision makers as they observe faithful parents modeling and instructing wise direction and decision making on their behalf. And with this kind of training, spoiled and indulged are words you'll never hear used to describe them.

7

Secret 7

Great Parents Work to Be Great Communicators

Have you ever thought about how you talk to your children? You know, really thought about some of your statements, questions, or expressions?

Much of what a parent says to a child is "maintenance talk." "Do this," "Do that," "Get dressed," "Wash up," "Put your toys away," "Brush your teeth." We end up sounding like military drill sergeants barking out orders rather than engaging in real communication. No wonder a child becomes "parent deaf."

What would it be like to be on the inside of your child's brain to see how your words really registered? It's not always easy getting our message across to another adult, let alone to a child who thinks on a very different level. It might help to understand that in anything we say to someone else there are actually six components.

SIX MESSAGES OF VERBAL COMMUNICATION

First, there is the message you want to get across to the other person—what you really mean. Perhaps you've thought about it in advance, or maybe you just formulate it as you open your mouth. Either way, it may not come out the way you intended. So the second message is what you actually say. Now, let's turn to your child. The third message is what your child actually hears while filtering and processing the information, which leads to the fourth message—what your child thinks he or she hears! Uh-oh, now the possibility of misunderstanding increases.

> IF THE ISSUE IS NOT OPEN TO DISCUSSION OR DEBATE, DON'T PHRASE YOUR REQUEST AS A QUESTION.

The fifth message confuses matters even further—it's what your child says about what you said. Now it's back in your lap, because the sixth message is what you think your child said about what you said.

Discouraging? Rather. But it does illustrate why so often communication seems like such hard work. We want the other person not only to listen but also to understand what we mean. The old proverb, "Say what you mean and mean what you say," is a worthy goal, but not an easy one to achieve. It would be much easier if you spoke one another's language.

How often do you hear yourself saying to your child, "How many times do I have to tell you this?" or "What did I just say?" or "Didn't you hear what I just said?" Your child probably heard you, but he may not have understood you, since everyone takes in information in different ways.

In this chapter you will find a number of guidelines to help you communicate more effectively with your child. Perhaps you're already following some of them, but some may come as a surprise.

Watch What You Say

Have you ever asked your child, "Can't you behave?" Most of us have. What is the logical answer to that question? "Yes, but do I really want to? Nah." Rephrasing your question might help, but you also need to consider whether your child really knows what "behaving" means. Some do, some don't. Maybe it would be better not to make this a question at all, but instead, use a statement. This question, after all, is not usually asked in a calm moment. It usually arises out of frustration over the fact that your child isn't behaving like you want him to. A better approach would be to spell out what behavior you expect: "I want you to behave now and that means ..."

There's another question we've all used: "Are you going to stop it?" The answer is obvious when the behavior continues! Again, this is not the time to ask a question. Your child is not the one to determine whether he is going to stop this or that. That's your job, and you need to make that clear. "I want you to stop right now," spoken in a calm, but firm, voice will net much better results.

Say What You Mean

"What do you think you're doing?" is a request to knock off whatever it is that is occurring. You're not really asking for clarification, reasons, or a defense. Asking this question is an invitation to engage in a fruitless discussion that won't affect the behavior. If the issue is not open to discussion or debate, don't phrase your request as a question.

"You're driving me up the wall!" This may not be a question, but think what it communicates to the child: You've just admitted to her that she's pushed a button. In essence, you've just told her, "You are powerful!" Is that what you wanted? No way! You really meant, "Your behavior needs to change"—but that's not the main message she's coming away with. It helps to talk to your child before you get to this place.

When you make a clear statement rather than implying something through a question you are more likely to get the response you want. Any parent knows what is meant by all these phrases, but we can't assume that a child does.[1]

Do you ever find yourself repeating questions or commands? There's a message in repetitions as well. You may mean "You didn't listen" or "You didn't hear me" or "You didn't understand me." It's quite possible, though, that the message your child gets is "I don't have to respond the first time she says something."

Children are quick to catch on. I've overheard one child say to another, "Don't you have to go now? Your mom's calling you." The other one replies, "No, not yet. Not until her voice gets louder and she puts her hands on her hips. That's about the fifth time she'll say it, and that's when she means it."

What are your repetition, tone of voice, and body language telling your child? Is the right message being communicated?

USE WORDS YOUR CHILD UNDERSTANDS

We tend to use words very freely with children. We know what we mean when we say, "Time is getting away from us" or "We're wasting time" or "We need to stretch our time." But do they?

It's also important to be specific. How often have you said, "It's been a rotten morning" when the reality was that your child acted up, was late, or just plain messed up. The word *it* casts the blame on the morning, and lets your child off the hook, even in his own mind. You have given the message that what happened was beyond your child's control. Say what you really mean.

You will be faced with a universal temptation. It's built into all of us parents. When we hear something from our children that we think is not accurate, we correct, explain, or give an excuse. There is a gag rule on these three possibilities no matter how wrong you think your child's version may be. When you do that your child hears the message, "You're wrong." She won't want to share how she really feels. You're not called to be a critic of your child's accuracy, but a listener to feelings.[2]

Don't Use Clichés

You know them all, because you heard them from your parents. "This is for your own good." "When you have your own children you'll know what I'm talking about." "Someday you'll see the wisdom of all this."

Those particular well-worn phrases are used to justify unpopular decisions—but why bother? We don't need to give a defense. And besides, it doesn't help.

Children may not respond to clichés with their eyes glazed over, but they do probably roll their eyes and mouth all the words along with us. They've heard it before and will hear it again, and it has ceased to have any meaning.

And what about, "Just wait till your father gets home" or "Stop crying or I'll give you something to cry about." Do they really inspire a behavior change? If you really need to say something, find a fresh way to say it that has a chance of getting results.

MAKE YOUR REQUEST CLEAR

Do you ever use the words "Could you …" when asking your child to do something? Probably. We all have. You're asking your child to do a task, to complete a project, to take an action. But when you use the word *could* or *can*, you're questioning their competence.

Instead of a request for help, it becomes a query of capability. It's not direct enough. If you're truly asking for your child's compliance, say "Will you …" instead. It's a request clearly stated.[3] Be certain, though, that "no" would be an acceptable answer. If not, don't ask a question—issue an order!

TRY TO MATCH YOUR CHILD'S LEARNING STYLE

Have you ever asked your child, "How many times do I have to tell you this?" or "What did I just say?" or "Didn't you hear what I just said?" Your child probably heard you, but he may not have understood you, since everyone takes in information in different ways.

Sometimes we parents become frustrated with our children because what we say just doesn't seem to connect with them. If so, it could be that all we need to do is adjust our presentation a bit in order to match our children's learning styles.

There are primarily three ways of taking in information. We all use all of them in varying degrees, but one of them is generally the way we learn best. Which of these is your learning style? Which do you think is your child's?

Some people are auditory. They learn best by listening to verbal instructions, and they remember best by forming the sounds of words—in other words, by repeating the information.

Others are visual. They learn by seeing, watching, and reading. They use strong visual associations in order to remember things.

Others are kinesthetic. They learn best by becoming physically involved with the material. They remember better when they have a chance to do something with what they're learning.

LISTEN TO THE WORDS YOUR CHILD USES

As you listen to a person talk, the words she uses often express her learning style.

The visual person uses phrases such as these:

- I see what you're saying.
- That looks good to me.
- I'm not too clear on this right now.
- This is still a bit hazy to me.
- Boy, when they asked that question, I just went blank.
- That sheds a new light on the problem.
- Do you see where I'm coming from?

The auditory person uses terms such as these:

- That rings a bell with me.
- It sounds real good to me.
- I hear you.
- I'm trying to tune in to what you're saying.
- Listen to this new idea.

- I had to ask myself.
- Now, that idea clicks with me.

The kinesthetic person will use phrases such as these:

- I can't get a handle on this.
- I've got a good feeling about this project.
- Can you get in touch with what I'm saying?
- It's easy to flow with what they're saying.
- I don't grasp what you're trying to do.
- This is a heavy situation.

Listen to the words your child uses. The great parent recognizes that they are clues to the most effective way to communicate with him or her.

Children vary in another way. Some will be expanders when they talk, giving all sorts of information and detail. It's as though they give you a full novel-length story. They can handle parents giving them lots of details. But if your child is a condenser, one who gives the bottom line or summations, he will do best getting a condensed version of the information you want to impart. If you give him the long version, after a few lines he'll tune you out. He doesn't need all the information you think he needs. Give him a little and let him ask for more if he needs it. When you talk with a condenser, try to say what you have to say in ten words or less. That may be a challenge, but you'll get better results.

Some children are what I call "straight arrow" in their thinking and communicating style. They like things presented, not only in bottom-line fashion, but sequentially. If you happen to be a "rambler" in your thinking and speaking style (and there's nothing wrong with either style), you could lose the straight arrow. Ramblers tend to not always identify the topic when they begin talking. They may not finish a complete thought or sentence, and they'll likely take detours around the barn a few times before returning to the topic. Two ramblers understand one another and connect easily, but a straight arrow is lost and frustrated. If your child is a rambler, try using the phrase "Let's think about all the possibilities." Unlike the straight arrow, ramblers are not overwhelmed by this suggestion, but inspired.[4]

It's possible for you, no matter what your style, to adapt to your child's style and be heard.

A CHILD LEARNS EARLY TO JAB AT HER PARENTS WITH WORDS, USING THEM AS A TOOL TO REVISE YOUR RESPONSES OR GET HER OWN WAY.

DON'T LET WORDS BECOME WEAPONS

Every person ever born on this planet comes equipped with one of the most powerful weapons ever created—a mouth. And the ammunition? Words. Just look at what Scripture says about their power:

> A bit in the mouth of a horse controls the whole horse. A small rudder on a huge ship in the hands of a skilled captain sets a course in the face of the strongest winds. A word out of your mouth may seem of no account, but it can accomplish nearly anything—or destroy it!
>
> It only takes a spark, remember, to set off a forest fire.... By our speech we can ruin the world, turn harmony to chaos, throw mud on a reputation, send the whole world up in smoke and go up in smoke with it, smoke right from the pit of hell.

> This is scary: You can tame a tiger, but you can't tame a tongue—it's never been done. The tongue runs wild, a wanton killer. With our tongues we bless God our Father; with the same tongues we curse the very men and women he made in his image. Curses and blessings out of the same mouth! (James 3:3–10 MSG)

> Do you see a man who is hasty in his words? There is more hope for a [self-confident] fool than for him. (Prov. 29:20 AB)

> If you want a happy, good life, keep control of your tongue, and guard your lips. (1 Peter 3:10 TLB)

> A word fitly spoken ... is like apples of gold in settings of silver. (Prov. 25:11 AB)

A child learns early to jab at her parents with words, using them as a tool to revise your responses or get her own way. "I won't!" "No!" "You're mean!" "You're unfair!" "You're not a good mom." "You're so stupid." "I don't care." "You can't make me." "I want new parents." "I hate you."

What do these words elicit in us? Anger, fear, frustration, guilt, powerlessness—you may feel like resigning, shipping your child to another country for a week, or showing him who is really in charge. When your buttons are pushed, though, you have an opportunity to examine your emotional response and decide whether it's valid or whether you're being had.

I'm a bass fisherman. I try to throw out a lure or plastic worm or spinner bait that will cause a bass to react. Many times a fish strikes, not out of hunger, but because he feels threatened since I invaded his territory. It's a wise bass that ignores my offering and doesn't get hooked. If the fish ignores me enough, I'll go away. Like that bass, you have the choice of ignoring the bait and responding in a way that will help solve the problem.

The author of *Kids, Parents, and Power Struggles* suggests that whenever your child launches a verbal attack, you respond like this: "Stop, that's bulldozing. I think you have something very important to say, but when you say it that way I stop listening. You can say it in a way that persuades me to listen."[5]

SELF-TALK IS WHAT YOU TELL YOURSELF—THE WORDS YOU SAY TO YOURSELF ABOUT YOURSELF, YOUR CHILDREN, YOUR EXPERIENCES, THE PAST, THE FUTURE, GOD.

One parent said, "I'd like to think I could do that, but once my button is pushed, I reach back into my emotional responses and let it fly. I want to show my child who's in charge."

I replied, "So, you're saying the emotion of your child is determining how you respond, is that right?"

"Yeah, I guess it is."

"And you're wanting to show who's in charge?"

"Yes, I am."

"So who is in charge if you let your child determine how you act?"

Make no mistake, that's one answer that is abundantly clear to your child!

Our kids aren't the only ones who inflict wounds with their words, though. How do you tend to talk to your child? It might help to commit to memory the following Scriptures:

- Careless words stab like a sword, but wise words bring healing. (Prov. 12:18 NCV)

- Patient people have great understanding, but people with quick tempers show their foolishness. (Prov. 14:29 NCV)
- Those who are careful about what they say keep themselves out of trouble. (Prov. 21:23 NCV)
- Do you see people who speak too quickly? There is more hope for a foolish person than for them." (Prov. 29:20 NCV)

WATCH YOUR OWN SELF-TALK

Every day we carry on conversations with ourselves. It's all right. It doesn't mean we're odd or on the verge of spacing out. It's completely normal to talk to oneself.

But are you aware of these facts:

- Most of your emotions—such as anger, depression, guilt, worry—are initiated and escalated by your self-talk?
- The way you behave toward your child is determined by your self-talk and not by his or her behavior?
- What you say, and how you say it, is a direct expression of what you say to yourself?

Self-talk is what you tell yourself—the words you say to yourself about yourself, your children, your experiences, the past, the future, God.

Self-talk, or your inner conversation, is not an emotion or feeling, and it is not an attitude. However, repetitious self-talk turns into attitudes, feelings, values, and beliefs.

Many of your thoughts are automatic. Thoughts slide into your consciousness so smoothly that you don't sense their entrance. Many of them are stimulated by your storehouse of memories and experiences. This storehouse is filled with those things you concentrate on most.

The Scriptures have much to say about our thought life. The words *think*, *thought*, and *mind* are used over three hundred times in the Bible. Proverbs 23:7 says, "As he thinks within himself, so he is" (NASB).

Often the Scriptures refer to our hearts as the source of our thoughts:

- The mind of the [uncompromisingly] righteous studies how to answer, but the mouth of the wicked pours out evil things. (Prov. 15:28 AB)
- But the things that come out of the mouth come from the heart, and these make a man 'unclean.' For out of the heart come evil thoughts, murder, adultery, sexual immorality, theft, false testimony, slander. (Matt. 15:18–19)

God knows the content of our thoughts: "All the ways of a man are pure in his own eyes, but the Lord weighs the spirits (the thoughts and intents of the heart)" (Prov. 16:2 AB). So, how are your thoughts? Do you see the connection between what's occurring inside you and what you say? It's something to become very aware of for the health of all your relationships.

There is good news: Our thought lives can come under the control of the Holy Spirit. First Peter 1:13 tells us to gird up our minds. This takes mental exertion, putting out of our minds anything that would hinder progress in our parenting. God's Word tells us what to concentrate on: "Finally, brethren, whatever is true, whatever is honorable, whatever is right, whatever is pure, whatever is lovely, whatever is of good repute, if there is any excellence and if anything worthy of praise, dwell on these things" (Phil. 4:8 NASB).

One of the concerns I keep hearing from parents was best put by this mother: "I know I need to change, I want to change, but I'm just not sure how to do it. You say it's possible—all right, how?"

You've made a good start by asking those questions. The basic answer is work. You've got to be willing to put forth effort and change will occur. Here are some steps to take:

1. Keep an interaction log. Write down accounts of some of your troublesome interactions with your child. It will help you see where things went wrong.
2. How would you describe what you say to your child? Are there patterns? Are you saying too much, too little? Are your questions really questions? Do you sound like your own mom and dad?
3. Use the tape recorder. Leave it on during the prime interactive times—before and right after school, dinner, bedtime. What did you learn?
4. Are there any character traits beginning to develop in your child that concern you? Is your child stuck anywhere? Write down your concerns and consider whom you could ask for help.
5. Don't be afraid to ask others what they have observed in your interactions with your children. You may not like what you hear, but if you really want to change be open to the perspectives of other trusted adults.
6. Go back through this book and write down every suggestion you think can make a difference in your life. Each day for the next thirty days reread these suggestions out loud. If the suggestion necessitates a new type of response, write it out and rehearse it aloud so you become accustomed to hearing your new expression.

Change is possible. But be patient—you didn't develop your communication nor your parenting styles overnight. Pray for God's wisdom and guidance as you grow in becoming a great parent. With God's help, you can make it happen.

8

Secret 8

Great Parents Know How to Use the Tools of Listening and Timing

One of the greatest gifts a great parent can give to a child is the gift of listening to him. As James 1:19 tells us, we are to be ready listeners. "Everyone should be quick to listen, slow to speak, and slow to become angry." Perhaps nowhere is this more important than between parents and their children.

Listening is a gift of spiritual significance that you can learn to give to others. In Proverbs we read, "The hearing ear and the seeing eye—the Lord has made both of them" (Prov. 20:12 AB). When you listen to your child, you give him a sense of importance, hope, and love that he may not receive any other way. Through listening, we nurture and validate the feelings of others, especially when they are experiencing difficulties in life. Consider these Scriptures:

- I love the LORD, because He hears my voice and my supplications. Because He has inclined His ear to me, therefore I shall call upon Him as long as I live. (Ps. 116:1–2 NASB)
- Anyone who answers without listening is foolish and confused. (Prov. 18:13 NCV)
- Any story sounds true until someone tells the other side and sets the record straight. (Prov. 18:17 TLB)
- The wise man learns by listening; the simpleton can learn only by seeing scorners punished. (Prov. 21:11 TLB)
- Call to me and I will answer you and tell you great and unsearchable things you do not know. (Jer. 33:3)
- Let every man be quick to hear [a ready listener]. (James 1:19 AB)

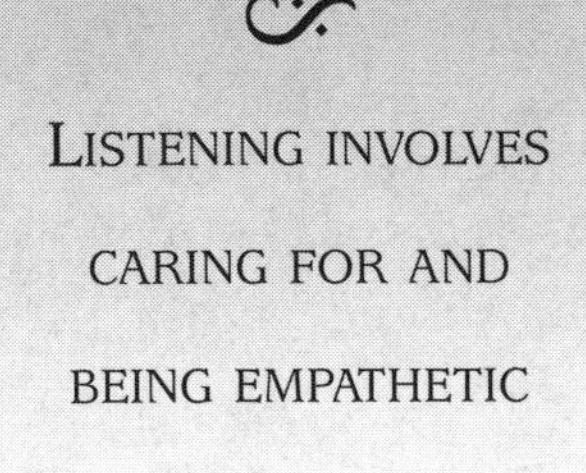

What do we mean by listening? What do we mean by hearing? Is there a difference? Hearing involves gaining content or information for your own purposes. Listening involves caring for and being empathetic toward your child. Hearing means you are focused on what is going on inside you during the conversation. Listening means that you are trying to understand the feelings of your child and are listening for his or her sake. That's a big difference, and children can easily pick up on it!

This is what listening really means:

1. Listening means that you're not thinking ahead to what you are going to say while your son or

daughter is still talking. You're not busy formulating your response. Instead, you're concentrating on what is being said, and you're putting into practice Proverbs 18:13: "Anyone who answers without listening is foolish and confused" (NCV).

2. Listening means that you're simply taking in completely what is being said, without judging what is said or how he or she is saying it. If you don't like your child's tone of voice or the words he's using and you react on the spot, you may miss the meaning—and children do use tones that push our buttons! Perhaps your child hasn't said it in the best way, but why not listen and then come back later to discuss the proper wording and tone of voice? Address your child's message first; save the means of communicating for later. Acceptance doesn't mean that you agree with the content of what your child says.
3. Listening means being able to repeat what your child has said and express what you think he or she was feeling while speaking to you. Real listening implies having an interest in your child's feelings and opinions and attempting to understand those feelings from his or her perspective. When we can do that, we've connected in a positive way.

Listening is a learnable skill. Your mind and ears can be taught to hear more keenly; your eyes can be taught to see more clearly. You can also learn to hear with your eyes and see with your ears. Jesus said: "Therefore I speak to them in parables; because while seeing they do not see, and while hearing they do not hear, nor do they understand. In their case the prophecy of Isaiah is being fulfilled, which says, 'You will keep on hearing, but will not understand; you will keep on seeing, but will not perceive; for the heart of this people has become dull, with their ears they scarcely hear, and they have closed their eyes otherwise they would see with their eyes, hear with their ears, and understand with their heart and return, and I would heal them'" (Matt. 13:13–15 NASB).

Let your ears hear and see.

Let your eyes see and hear.

There are many reasons why people listen. Some parents listen for facts, information, and details for their own use. Others listen because they feel sorry for the person. Some listen to gossip because they revel in the juicy story of another person's failures or difficulties. On occasion, people listen out of obligation, out of necessity, or to be polite. Some who listen are nothing more than voyeurs who have an incessant need to pry and probe into other people's lives.

Great parents listen because they care.

I've heard people say, "When I listen, it seems to cause the other person to just talk and talk and talk. Why?" Perhaps initially it does, but if you remain perfectly silent, you create such a tension within the person speaking that he or she begins to back off.

Why do we listen to our children? Partly because we've been taught or admonished to do so. But there are five basic reasons why we ought to listen:

1. To understand our children
2. To enjoy them
3. To learn something from our children (such as their learning language)
4. To give help, assistance, or comfort to them
5. To show our love to our children

COMMON OBSTACLES TO COMMUNICATION

In order for caring listening to happen, we need to be aware of some of the common obstacles to communication.

Defensiveness is one. We miss the message if our minds are busy thinking up a rebuttal, excuse, or exception to what our children are saying. And it causes other problems as well.

There are a variety of defensive responses. Perhaps we reach a premature conclusion. "All right, I know just what you're going to say. We've been through this before and it's the same old thing." Maybe it is, but maybe it isn't. Wait until you find out.

We may read into our children's words our own expectations or even project onto them what we would say in the same situation. This isn't true listening. Your child isn't you. Don't assume you understand; make sure you understand.

Listening is more than just hearing what someone else is saying—it's giving sharp attention to what your child is sharing with you. Often your child is sharing more than he is saying. We must listen to the total person, not just the words spoken. Listening requires an openness to whatever is being shared: feelings, attitudes, or concerns, as well as words. Listening also means putting yourself in a position to respond to whatever is being shared with you.

Listening is an expression of love. It involves caring enough to take seriously what your child is communicating. When you listen lovingly, you invite him into your life as a guest.

When your child knows you hear him, he will trust you and feel safe with you. And if you are a good listener, he will be more apt to invite you into his life in return. He also learns through your example to respond openly and lovingly to what you share with him.

Remember, there is a difference between listening and hearing. The goal of hearing is to gain content or information for your own purposes. When you hear, you are concerned about what is going on inside you during the conversation. You are tuned in to your own responses, thoughts, and feelings.

With our children, we want to be listeners. We want to care for and empathize with our children. When we listen, we want to try to understand the thoughts and feelings of our children. We are listening for their sakes, not our own.

LOOK YOUR CHILDREN IN THE EYES WHEN YOU TALK WITH THEM. EVEN A WINK TELLS THEM, "I LOVE YOU."

Good listening starts with silence. Even when your child has done something wrong, the more you listen to him, the more information you'll have to help you understand what happened. It may be quite different from what you think! The younger the child, the less commentary your child needs from you. It's easy for you to put thoughts into words, but it can be a laborious experience for a preschooler. Don't fill in their words for them or try to hurry them along. Give younger children plenty of time to express themselves.

When your child shares a problem with you or a critical concern, don't immediately give advice. Learn to use questions and you'll end up learning so much more. Here are a few examples that can be adapted for different ages:

- What was going on in your mind when you did that?
- Have you thought of what else you could have done?
- Did you hope things would turn out this way or …?
- What do you think you could do to make things better?

- What do you think could be done to resolve this?
- If you were me what would you do now?[1]

Communicate by Touching and Looking

There are other ways to communicate that are very effective—without words. We say so much without ever using words. Touching and hugging convey more than can be said with any words. Our mentally disabled son, Matthew, was only eighteen months old intellectually when he died at the age of twenty-two. We would touch him affectionately and hug him a lot. But for years he never hugged back. It was a one-sided display of affection. When he was about fifteen, something happened in his development and training. Once or twice a year he would reach out with his arms and put them around us when we gave him a hug. In one way it wasn't a lot, and yet in another it meant the world to us. Don't go without touching in your home.

Another way you connect with your children is with your eyes. Look your children in the eyes when you talk with them. Even a wink tells them "I love you." Your eyes convey the silent language of love. Make up secret signals that give you a unique way to communicate a special message that only your family knows and understands.

Pick Your Time to Communicate

In Proverbs 15:23 (NLT) we read, "It is wonderful to say the right thing at the right time." *When* you talk with your child can be just as important as *how* you talk with her. When is the best time of day to talk with your child? When is she most responsive? When she's happy? When she's sad? When she's well rested? For many children, it's "ouch" time.

What is "ouch" time? It's when your child comes to you with either a physical or emotional ouch. How you respond at such a crucial time can reinforce independence or dependence. What do you say, for instance, when your eight-year-old trips while skating and skins her knee? Here are four possibilities:

"Oh you poor thing. You hurt your little knee. Now, you come into the house, lie down, and let Mommy fix it for you. You rest awhile and I'll bring you your favorite snack." With this response, she learns how to get attention and special treatment.

"You're so clumsy. I told you you're too young to try that. Get into the house and put those skates away. We'll wait until you've got better balance. Listen to me next time." This is a good way to make your child feel inadequate.

"Oh, don't worry, honey. It wasn't your fault. Those aren't the best skates. And that stupid sidewalk has all those cracks and bumps in it. The city needs to fix things like that so you won't trip." This poor child is learning to blame whatever is handy. He's not learning to take responsibility.

"Jordan, it's just a scratch. I'll put a Band-Aid on it now, and we'll clean it up later when you take a bath. Go back and skate some more. Everyone falls down when they're learning. I know I did. I had a sore bottom for days one time. You're doing well and pretty soon you won't be falling down."

This response is realistic and keeps the event in perspective. This was a supportive teaching response and an example of great parenting in action.[2]

Mealtime can be another good time to talk. True, it can be hectic or a delight! But with a little effort and planning, it can also be a wonderful time for family discussions. One family said, "We have to work at having our dinner together four to five nights a week. There is no TV on, no video games at the table, the phone is off the hook or all ringers are off, no beepers are on, and no one leaves early. We talk and sometimes each person shares what was important to him or her that day. Other times questions are taped to the bottom of the plate and each one can ask another person the question on that piece of paper. We also have a rule that when someone is talking no one can interrupt."

Another family had a tradition with their three sons. Once a month they had a round-table discussion at breakfast. Each person had five minutes to tell what was going on in his life and how he felt about it. No interruptions. If someone needed another five minutes he could have it. It was his or her own personal time.

Make the Most of Your Moments Together

Even without planned times of communication, there are spontaneous moments in every family when a connection can take place. These moments may include in the morning, in the car, after school, and bedtime.

What do you talk about in the morning? Are your first words a positive, pleasant greeting or a grumpy, task-oriented set of orders? What occurs at this time can set the tone for the rest of the day. It's easy to fall into the trap of barking commands or complaints like these:

"You forgot your books."

"You're going to be late again."

"Do I have to tell you every day to get your coat?"

"Eat your breakfast; you need to have energy."

There are alternative ways of communicating the same messages. Try these:

"I saw your books on the piano. You might want to put them by the front door now."

"Let's both watch the clock; then neither of us will be late today."

"I read the weather report, and it's going to be cold. I'm wearing my warm jacket; are you wearing yours?"

"You look sleepy. A good breakfast might help wake you up."

Another time for quality conversation seems to happen while you're driving. It may be one of the few moments when everyone is together going in the same direction, if even for a short amount of time. For whatever reason, children seem more prone to talk to you in the car, especially when all the radios, hand-held games, and CD players with headphones are off.[3]

It's also a great time for parents to listen and learn, especially when your child has a friend along. Your child will often share things with his or her friend as if you are invisible. Make a note of things to talk with your child about at a later time or interject into their conversation if it seems appropriate.

What occurs during the first four minutes after the end of the school day between you and your child can set the tone for the rest of the evening. First, know if this is a good time to talk with your child. Some children need some down time and a snack before they are ready to talk. Just as working parents may need to unwind when they first get home, so do some children.

Initially you may feel that your child has little to say. As one parent complained, "I ask, 'How was your day?' and all I get is 'OK' or 'fine' or 'boring.' And 'What did you do?' 'Stuff' or 'Nothing.'"

Actually this child did answer the questions. Some creative rephrasing may help. For example, you could make observations rather than always grilling your child. "You look tired today." "You look like you had a special day." "You look a bit discouraged." Asking questions that are more specific can also open up communication: "What did you learn in (art, social studies) today?" "How did you do on your (science, spelling, math) test?" And, of course, the physical contact is a must![4]

Bedtime is an occasion when a child can unwind and might be prompted to share things she wouldn't share during the day. In fact, many times she will say more than she really wants to just to stall for another ten minutes! This is often a good time to sit on her bed and ask, "What were the good times and best times of today? What were the bad times?" Parents can then pray with their children in a very specific way, ending their children's day on a note of love and hope.

SPEND FIVE MINUTES A DAY ALONE, AWAY FROM EVERYONE ELSE AND ALL INTERRUPTIONS, WITH EVERY CHILD IN YOUR FAMILY EVERY SINGLE DAY.

GIVE YOUR CHILD A TIME TO SHARE

Communication includes many elements. It involves talking, but it also includes silence. Often what is said can be the most significant part of an interaction between parent and child. Sometimes the silence is good. It allows time for reflection and emotional closeness, and it may mean you've refrained from saying something better left unsaid. But other times silence can be negative. Have you ever considered what might be left unsaid between you and your child? Perhaps as a parent you feel that you can and have said everything you want. Can your child tell you "anything"? Does he feel as though he has permission to share? Do you show as much interest in your child as a person as you do in his activities, in what he's created, drawn, or written?

The authors of *What Did I Just Say?* have suggested that every parent and child needs five minutes a day of genuine, intense communication. You may think that's not very much time and that you already give that much or more. But do we? The problem is most of us tend to communicate on the run, doing two or three things or activities at the same time. Can you think of the last time you and your child sat down and talked face-to-face? No TV on, no computer, no games, no food—just the two of you, eyeball to eyeball. Many have difficulty remembering. Here's what you can do:

Spend five minutes a day alone, away from everyone else and all interruptions, with every child in your family every single day. Don't allow any other activities to go on. During this time your child gets to talk to you about anything he or she would like to talk about. You are to listen—not talk, not interpret, not correct your child's version. Your job is to listen, understand, and validate how your child feels about what is being said. Why do this? It costs nothing, takes little time, connects you to your child on a regular basis, builds a calming effect, promotes open, honest sharing, and draws the two of you closer together.

You begin by letting your child know that you are going to begin a special time for the two of you each day. Let him know he can say whatever he thinks and feels and you'll be there to listen. You may get some resistance or smart remarks about this time. That's all right. Don't get hooked into a battle. Just do it.

Following the rules is very important. Private time means this time belongs only to your child. Bathroom, phone, beeper, other kids, spouse, dog—none of these can distract you. And this needs to be done one-on-one. Both parents need their own time with each child. It's possible. A friend of mine gave one hour of private time to each of his five children each week for years. It did wonders for them.

The five minutes spent each day is essential. If you have to miss, pick it up the next day. If you are detained, it can be done via plan B—over the phone. But the same rules apply—the child shares what he wants. Avoid factual reports of games or outings—just ask how your child feels. And this is not a democratic process! Just because the child gets five minutes does not mean the parent gets equal time. It's your child who needs to be understood and accepted—you have that need too, but your child is not the person to meet it.

If your child just wants to sit silently with you for five minutes, that's all right. Don't interrupt what she's thinking. She could be talking to you in her mind. Some children might take days or weeks to open up. Just don't fill the silence with words. This is the time for your child to share whatever has been building up. She does, however, need to do it respectfully.[5]

BE POSITIVE AND APPRECIATIVE

Some parents seem to be on a mission. They feel called to catch their children doing something wrong, disobeying, or failing to follow through. What parents look for they will find. These are also parents who usually jump all over their children for the discovered mistakes. This approach only serves to reinforce those mistakes, guaranteeing they will recur.

I have two golden retrievers. They are wonderful family dogs. I've invested time and attention in both their care and training. Both Sheffield and Aspen go out and retrieve the paper. We will drop or throw an item to be discarded on the floor and say "trash" and one or the other dog will pick it up, take it, and place it in the trash can. I can tell Sheffield to go get his bowl from the drawer and he'll run into the bedroom, pull open the drawer, bring me the bowl, and then go back and bring his sack of food. I can take Aspen out without a leash and walk a half mile with her right next to my left side. A few times I say, "Heel," and she does because that's what she's been trained to do. These aren't super dogs; they were just trained. How? In their training, when they didn't do something right, nothing was said, we just tried it again.

When they do something right, that's when they hear about it—big time! They receive verbal praise, a touch, a tummy rub, or a pat on the head. In some ways, people are a lot like dogs. When they do something right, they need to hear about it—big time! When they mess up, don't reinforce it by going over the details, but focus on what they will do differently next time.

All of us need to be recognized for who we are and what we have done. Appreciation imparts a feeling of significance. Josh McDowell describes the importance of appreciation in one of his books:

> It's funny how one little phrase can bring a concept or principle to life. I was sold on giving my kids unconditional acceptance, but I had been struggling with learning how to appreciate them. It isn't that I never praised them for what they did; it was simply a matter of praising them after I was sure that I had corrected all the things they had done wrong. Naturally, because kids have a tendency to make mistakes, it was just too easy to find them doing things wrong. Mix that with their intuitive ability to perceive that the best way to get my attention was to do something wrong and I had a real problem.
>
> One side of me had been trying to accept my children, and the other side had been trying to correct them for doing things wrong. It was no wonder

that I often felt a little schizophrenic! But all that changed when I turned the emphasis upside down. Instead of concentrating on what they were doing wrong, I started to make a conscious effort to look for what they were doing right. My new goal was to find at least two things about each child that I could appreciate every day, and then to be sure to compliment each child on what I saw.

I'm not sure my children noticed any "overnight difference," but I know I did. My whole perspective on parenting changed.

I would look over and see Kelly studying and then stop a moment to say, "Honey, I appreciate the way you study." When I saw Sean taking out the trash, I would stop him and say, "Sean, thanks for remembering to take the trash out."

I'd find little Katie picking up her toys, and I'd say, "Katie, sweetheart, Daddy really appreciates how you take care of your toys."

Another thing I began to do was try to find all the children in the same general area—our family room for example—and stand in the middle of all of them for an "appreciation session." In this case, I wouldn't necessarily say anything out loud, but I would consciously stop for three minutes to ask myself, How many things can you appreciate about your kids if you stop to think about it right now? Then I would try to mentally list fifteen or twenty things I appreciated about the four of them. That meant finding about four or five items per child, but I always made it well within the three-minute time limit I set for myself.

THE WAY YOU COMMUNICATE WITH YOUR CHILD CAN CHANGE YOUR RELATIONSHIP, AND IT CAN ALSO GO A LONG WAY TOWARD CHANGING BEHAVIOR.

> This little exercise helped remind me of just how much I have to be thankful for about my kids, and it kept me primed for saying appreciative things at the proper time. You see, it isn't a matter of not being able to find things to appreciate about your kids; what it's all about is programming yourself to speak up and tell your kids what you see—to give them honest praise for their effort.[6]

There's another principle to follow when you give your corrective requests to your children. Make them positive rather than negative. It's easy to tell a child what to stop doing. That's like second nature with some of us. Have you found yourself making statements like "I want you to stop being rough to the cat" or "I want you to stop talking" or "I want you to stop arguing with me"?

If not these statements I'm sure you have your own list of "I want you to stop ..." statements. The emphasis in these kinds of statements is on what is negative. What you don't want to happen. Instead, tell your child what you want her to do: "I want you to be gentle and kind to your cat" or "I want you to be quiet now"or "I want you to do what I say instead of playing Nintendo now."

A parent asked me, "Norm, I've changed my requests like this, but sometimes I get an argument. I get resistance or noncompliance. She wants to keep playing on the computer and tells me she doesn't want to stop." What could this parent say? What would you say?

You could acknowledge her desire to keep playing, but then begin using the broken record approach. It goes something like this: "I understand you want to keep playing, but I want you to come get ready for church." No matter what response you get back from your child, just repeat in a calm, soft voice, "I want you to come now and get ready for church." Learn to use "I want," coupled with what you want, not what she wants to keep doing. And again, don't give reasons. It's amazing, but eventually she will give in.

The way you communicate with your child can change your relationship, and it can also go a long way toward changing behavior. Put some of the principles in this chapter to the test and see for yourself.

9

Secret 9

Great Parents Pay Attention to a Child's Emotions

Each day we all experience a variety of feelings. They may range from curiosity to surprise, from happiness to anger, from delight to despair—often within moments of each other. We've learned to cope with them, but sometimes they can be very confusing to our children.

What great parents know is that, just as we adults are often governed by our feelings, *emotions influence every part of a child's life.* They're like a sixth sense, monitoring his needs, making him aware of good and evil, and providing motivation and energy for growth and change. Emotions give a child the vigor and impetus for living. They help him understand himself and others, and they warn him when he's in danger—when his boundaries have been crossed or his rights are being violated. Emotions even help your child define his values. Emotions can impact every area of your child's life.

The Bible has a lot to say about feelings. From Genesis through Revelation, we read about God's emotions and those of the men, women, and children he created. According to Scripture, Christ experienced and expressed a wide range of feelings, including love, compassion, joy, fear, sorrow, disappointment, discouragement, frustration, hurt, rejection, loneliness, and anger. When God created us in his image, he gave us a mind, a will, and emotions. Some of us are overly aware of these feelings and some seem to be oblivious. Emotions may be positive or negative, pleasurable or painful; we can acknowledge them or ignore them. We can learn to use them constructively or allow them to control us. Emotions aren't optional, but how we choose to express them and respond to them is. Children have to learn healthy ways to do this, and the best way is by example from their parents.

EMOTIONS INFLUENCE EVERY PART OF A CHILD'S LIFE.

Some children never learn to understand, value, and deal with their emotions. They spend their entire lives struggling with and trying to overcome the consequences of unhealthy emotional habits. Many grow up emotionally handicapped. This contributes to a wide range of problems that complicate their lives and prevents them from becoming the responsible, healthy people God intended for them to be.

We may not always be aware of our emotions, but ignoring them can cause us serious problems. This is especially true with children.

When we take the time to help our children deal with their feelings, we're doing them a big favor. The way children learn to handle their feelings is fundamental to how happy they will be as adults.

Our children can learn at an early age to develop healthy emotional attitudes. As parents, we can communicate that in our families it is safe to experience and express feelings. We can give our kids a vocabulary for expressing what they feel and teach them to differentiate between experiencing and expressing emotions. And we can set goals for their emotional growth that shape the kinds of habits they develop.

When it comes to emotions, what your child needs more than anything is a love that is sometimes difficult to give—unconditional love. What will help your child feel loved is based more upon what you *do* than on what you *say*. Verbal expressions often mean more to an adult than to a child. A parent needs to convey love to his or her child in emotional and behavioral ways. If a child feels loved unconditionally, he will accept your guidance, instruction, and discipline much better.

Unconditional love means you love your child no matter what his assets, abilities, looks, quirks, defects, personality traits, who he reminds you of, and how he acts.

A child's emotions are sensitive, even fragile. How did your child gain his first impressions of the world around him? Through his feelings. It's as though he has an emotional antenna. This means parents are called to care for their children's emotional needs first before anything else.

Thinking Like a Child—Emotionally

Does your child think like you? No. Does your preschool or elementary child have the ability to solve problems and handle her emotions the way adults do? No. But we often expect her to. She can't reason as we do, but often we give adult reasons for doing things and then wonder why it didn't work.

Are there days when you don't feel loved? Probably, but do you conclude you'll *never* be loved? Probably not. But a child does.

If a child loses something, he may believe it's gone forever and there won't be a replacement.

If a child can't have her piece of cake now, she thinks, *I'll never get one.*

If a child didn't get a hit in a Little League game, he believes he'll never get one.

This is child-think. It's different from parent-think. And that's why your child may have such strong emotional responses. He's reacting emotionally, not logically. That's where he lives. And that's why all the reasoning in the world can't reassure him at times. Your listening empathy will.

Dr. Ross Campbell talks about children having an emotional tank. This tank represents your child's emotional needs—needs that can only be met with love, understanding, and kind discipline. Our goal as parents is to keep our children's tanks full. Keeping them full has two results in your child's life. About this emotional tank, Dr. Campbell said,

> First, it determines the emotional state of your child—whether he is anxious, content, angry, joyful, depressed, or happy. This concern is largely neglected in reactive parenting. Second, the level of the emotional tank also affects your child's behavior. It greatly influences his response to training and discipline; it largely determines whether he is obedient, disobedient, whiny, perky, playful, or withdrawn. The better you keep the emotional tank full, the more positive your child's feelings and his behavior will be.[1]

So, if you want your child be at his best, keep his emotional tank full. This is done through unconditional love. How can you express this in ways he understands? First, your child needs an abundance of eye contact. He says, "Look at me." He needs this often, even continually, and especially during positive interactions. He also needs physical contact, and not just when you hug and kiss. Touching, rubbing his head, scratching his back—all these things help fill his tank.

Focused attention is another way to express love. Your child needs your full, undivided attention. You listen, you're there, and you're available. The five minutes a day discussed in the communication chapter is an example of this.[2]

And unconditional love is expressed by parents when they train, set limits, discipline, and say no. When asked by a friend, "How do you know your parents love you?" one child answered, "Because they don't let me do everything I want to. They care enough to say no."

How do you respond to your own feelings or emotions? For many parents, emotions are not only confusing, but they're also a problem. Many of us were raised emotionally handicapped. We weren't given any help with our own emotional development, and what we don't feel comfortable with we tend to fear, avoid, or resist. Often we don't know how to respond to our own feelings, let alone our children's. And it's easy to respond to your child's emotions in such a way that they end up damaged.

In his helpful book, *The Heart of Parenting*, John Gottman talks about the response of either dismissing your child's feelings or disapproving of them. If you've ever responded in this way, don't be alarmed or hard on yourself. It's possible to change. It's important to make the effort, though, because parents who dismiss or disapprove of their children's emotions tend to respond in many unfortunate ways.

Their children's feelings may be treated as trivial, unimportant. The parent shows this by ignoring the feelings, disengaging from the child, or ridiculing the way the child feels.

These reactions are especially likely when the emotions are negative ones, because parents often see these as reflecting on themselves in some way. They think perhaps it means their children are maladjusted or weak. Some go to the extreme of believing any expression of negative emotions needs to be controlled and may be an indication of bad character traits. This is not great parenting.

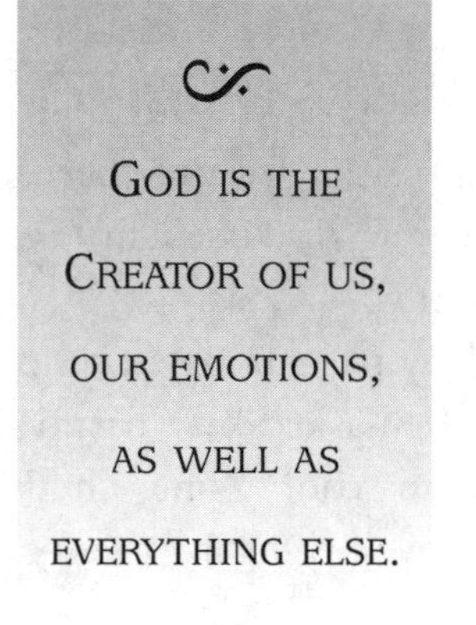

Parents who dismiss their children's emotions are saying something about themselves. When their children do reveal emotions, they feel uncomfortable, afraid, anxious, bothered, hurt, or even overwhelmed by the expression. They fear being out of control emotionally. Their natural response is, "Let's get past this as quickly as possible." No effort is given to understanding what it means. They miss a wonderful learning opportunity to practice problem-solving with their child—not to mention the feelings of closeness that arise from shared feelings.

If the parent disapproves of emotional expression, there's a strong controlling reaction. The immediate response is critical and judgmental. The parent might poke fun at a child's feelings or try to humiliate him. Discipline, reprimands, or even punishment may follow. This parent wants conformity to his standards no matter what.

The parent's inability to handle his own emotional life keeps him from helping his own child become more fully human.

Children who live with this response soon learn that feelings are not good, valid, healthy, or appropriate. Some children end up believing something is wrong with them because of the way they feel. So they fail to learn where their emotions originate, what they mean, and how to handle or express them.

You probably remember the tragic story of Jessica Pulroff, who died in a plane crash in 1996. She was the pilot of a single-engine Cessna and had just started her cross-country flight. At the age of seven, she would have been the youngest pilot ever to make the flight. Why would she try this? An article in the *New York Times* revealed a problem in the family. Jessica's mother would not let her use words like "fear," "scared," or "sadness." Her response to the reporters was, "Children are fearless. That's their natural state until adults ingrain fear in them." Her response to the *Times* after her daughter died was, "I know what people want. Tears. But I will not do that. Emotion is unnatural. There is something untruthful about it."[3]

As mentioned earlier, our second child, Matthew, was born profoundly mentally retarded. His presence in our lives was a wonderful blessing amidst all the losses and heartache. One of the lessons he taught me was to be fully human. I was like most men. I grew up emotionally handicapped. I didn't access my emotions; I ignored them; I didn't share them. But when Matthew entered my life I began to experience sensations I'd never experienced before. Often I couldn't control what I was feeling. To a man, that can be a bit scary. But through that time, I learned to accept my emotions. I learned to talk about them and describe them. And I learned to cry. I never apologize for my tears, for you never have to apologize for something that is a gift from God. And God is the Creator of us, our emotions, as well as everything else.

EMOTIONAL COACHING

There are some parents who go overboard and allow their children total freedom of emotional expression. There's no guidance, or comforting, or teaching, or limits. Just let them fly and everything will work itself out. That's sort of like running a blender with the lid off—and it's not the way a great parent approaches the child's emotional states.

There is a better way to respond. A new term, "emotional coaching," has been used to describe the way parents can teach their children to learn to trust their feelings, regulate their emotions, and solve problems on their own. What can a parent do that's healthy?

First, see your child's emotional expression (positive and negative) as your opportunity to connect emotionally. You can learn to be comfortable with your own emotions by doing this. Whatever your child shares won't be a threat. It's important to work at picking up on your child's emotional state even when it's not obvious. It's also important to respond to whatever emotions are shared, never to make fun of any of them, not to tell your child how she should feel, and not to try to fix every problem for your child.

When emotions are shared, view this as a teachable moment. This is the time to be empathetic, listening with your heart as well as with your head. Help your child put a name to the emotion, give guidance when needed, set limits, and teach acceptable, responsible expressions. This is one of your best opportunities to teach your child how to resolve problems.[4]

Dr. Gottman gives an example:

> Imagine, for a moment, a situation where eight-year-old William comes in from the yard, looking dejected because the kids next door have refused to play with him. His dad, Bob, looks up from his paper just long enough to say, "Not again! Look, William, you're a big kid now, not a baby. Don't get upset every time somebody gives the cold shoulder. Just forget about it. Call one of your buddies from school. Read a book. Watch a little TV."

Because children usually believe their parents' assessments, chances are William's thinking: "Dad's right. I'm acting like a baby, what's wrong with me? Why can't I just forget it like Dad says? I'm such a wimp. Nobody wants to be my friend."

Now imagine how William might feel if his father responds differently when he comes in. What if Bob puts down his newspaper, looks at his son, and says: "You look kind of sad, William. Tell me what's going on."

And if Bob listens, really listens with an open heart, perhaps William will come up with a different assessment of himself. This conversation might continue like this:

William: "Tom and Patrick won't let me play basketball with them."

Bob: "I'll bet that hurt your feelings."

William: "Yeah it did. It made me mad, too."

Bob: "I can see that."

William: "There's no reason why I can't shoot baskets with them."

Bob: "Did you talk to them about it?"

William: "Nah, I don't want to."

Bob: "What do you want to do?"

William: "I don't know. Maybe I'll just blow it off."

Bob: "You think that's a better idea?"

William: "Yea, 'cuz they'll probably change their minds tomorrow. I think I'll call one of my friends from school, or read a book. Maybe I'll watch some TV."[5]

Sometimes parents have asked, "What do I do to keep myself from telling him what to do or always trying to fix the problem? I'm not into this empathy stuff. I've never had my own feelings validated very much so I'm not real sure what to do or what to say."

What a great parent can do is to reflect back to your child what you think or feel he is feeling. If you were to read these phrases out loud each day for a month, you would begin to use them automatically.

- Are you kind of feeling …
- I'm picking up that you …
- If I'm hearing you correctly …
- To me it's almost like you are saying, 'I …'
- That kind of made you feel …
- The thing you feel most right now is sort of like …
- So, as you see it …
- I'm not sure I'm with you, but …
- I somehow sense that maybe you feel …
- I wonder if you're expressing a concern that …
- It sounds as if you're indicating you …
- You place a high value on …
- It seems to you …
- It appears to you …
- So, from where you sit …
- Sometimes you …
- It sounds like you're very much feeling …
- Your message seems to be, I …
- You appear …
- Listening to you, it seems as if …
- I gather …
- So your world is a place where you …
- You communicate a sense of …

You will need to let your child know what is a responsible way to express emotions and what isn't, what he can and cannot say, and what he can and cannot do.

- You can be mad, but you can't hit your brother.

- You can be upset at your sister, but you can't call her names.
- Any responses that hurt others or damage anything won't be tolerated.

In helping your child come up with a solution, use questions:

- What do you think you could do?
- What do you think might work?
- What have you tried before? Let's list the things that we've never tried before. Then you can choose one and see if it helps.
- If you were me, what do you think you would suggest?

If a solution doesn't work, talk about what happened and what they learned from the experience—and always talk about what they might be able to do differently the next time. Your children need lots of practice learning to make choices to find solutions. The younger a child learns to do this, the better it will be for everyone.

POWER STRUGGLES

Now, let's connect emotions to a common parent/child occurrence called power struggles. They're a part of every family. Have you ever had the experience of clearly and explicitly telling your child what to do, and then your child looks at you, smiles, and does exactly what you just told her not to do? If you haven't, rejoice—you're a rarity! And if you haven't, you probably will.

To make matters worse, many of the techniques that parents use don't seem to work. Sometimes the struggle becomes so intense that the parent folds and gives in to the child. And we know by now that can lead to indulgence. In her book, *Kids, Parents, and Power Struggles*, Mary Kurcinka describes the problem:

> YOUR CHILD'S ANGER BELONGS TO HIM OR HER; NO ONE ELSE.

> The parents have told me they've tried time-outs, reward systems, insisting that their kids 'toughen up' or stop being a 'baby,' and even spanking, but the struggles haven't stopped. I finally realized that the struggles continued because reward systems, time-outs, demands to 'not feel that way,' and spankings put a 'lid' on the behavior but failed to address the real fuel source behind them. As a result it was as though someone had put the lid back on a pot of boiling water but failed to turn down the heat. The water continued to boil and inevitably the lid popped off again.
>
> Emotions are the real fuel source behind power struggles. When you identify those emotions, you can select strategies that teach your kids what they are feeling and how to express those emotions more respectfully and suitably. The pot doesn't keep boiling over because ultimately the kids themselves learn to recognize and learn to turn it down.[6]

Have you considered the fuel source? It makes a difference. Often an emotion itself is not the real feeling. Has your child ever been angry? Of course. How have you responded? Did you say "Stop it" or "Don't be angry" or "That isn't nice to be angry" or "Go to your room until you calm down"? Probably we all have. Next time, try something like this: "It sounds like something is really bothering you. I'm wondering if you're frustrated about something or feeling hurt or perhaps afraid. Could you tell me about it?" What you're doing is getting at the cause of the anger since frustration, hurt, and fear are the three major causes.

Once the source is identified, how can you help your child with his anger?

1. Teach your child to deal with each hurt as it arises. Allowing hurts to accumulate makes them seem overwhelming—a mountain of hurts that cannot be moved.
2. Teach your child to take responsibility for his or her own anger. Your child's anger belongs to him or her; no one else is making him or her angry. The anger may or may not be appropriate, but it exists, and it must be reckoned with.
3. Teach your child to allow other people to have feelings also. Anger is seldom one-sided. Others have a right to feel angry too. Help your child see both sides of the conflict: "If someone has hurt you, it's possible that it's because you have hurt that person yourself."
4. Listen, receive, and accept your child's anger. Talking about anger helps to pinpoint its source and also may diffuse its intensity. Once your child is aware of where the anger came from, encourage him or her to let the anger go and focus on dealing with the cause of the hurt.
5. Show your child how to forgive. Explain why revenge is dangerous. Remind your child of what he or she would want if he or she were in the other person's shoes. And model forgiveness yourself.
6. Where appropriate, show your child how to face up to the person who is doing the hurting. This isn't always appropriate or even possible. The person may be too manipulative or reactive, and may even have moved away. But where possible, encourage and support your child in "facing up to the enemy."

7. Teach your child to seek reconciliation above self-gratification. Reconciliation restores broken relationships. If your child can learn to forgive and to be reconciled to those who cause hurt, he or she will have no problem dealing with life's major hurts.[7]

It's easy to get hooked into the unpleasantness of anger, but that won't make it disappear. Responding in the manner described lets your child know you understand and are willing to listen. It's worked for many. And in the same way, by going to the emotion underlying your child's resistance to you, the power struggle can be resolved. Not only that, when you commit yourself to take time (and it does take time!) to help your son or daughter to understand emotions and learn to label them, as well as learning healthy ways of expressing them, you build your child's emotional intelligence. It really works.

WE ARE ALL EMOTIONAL BEINGS

A friend of mine has a very unique way of helping his three boys understand and identify the underlying feeling behind anger. Since most anger is a secondary emotion and stems from either hurt, fear, or frustration, he will identify his own anger with "I'm feeling hurt right now because …" or "I'm feeling frustration and anger now because …" or "I'm feeling anger right now because you ran across the street and I was afraid of what might happen to you."

If we express anger without identifying our underlying feelings, which are likely to be love and concern, how would they ever know? By doing this and modeling the process, children learn a more accurate way of expressing what they are feeling.

For this to happen, both you and your child need to understand two things. One is that we were all created as emotional beings. This was God's plan. When David said in Psalm 139:14, "I am fearfully and wonderfully made," he was including his emotions. You can ignore them, deny them, or embrace them. One of the greatest gifts we can give our children is a healthy acceptance and understanding of their emotions. Naturally, one of the best ways is for our children to observe our own healthy expressions.

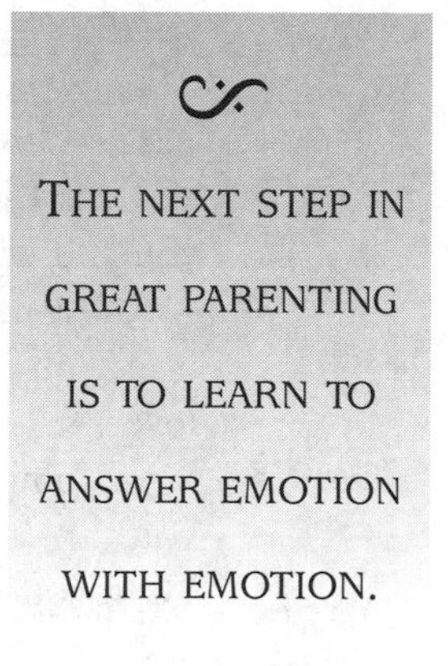

Instead of giving your child the name for his feeling, draw it out of him. If you say to your child, "You must be angry over that," will he admit to it or clam up? Often when you ask "action questions," like *who, what*, and *how*, a child learns to share his feelings because of your interest.

One of the worst questions to ask is "Why?" Most adults can't answer this question, let alone a child.

The other thing you and your child need to understand is how to identify and label your emotions.

For emotional closeness to occur, family members must learn to express emotion and communicate with feelings. This is difficult for many of us to do because we grew up without a "feeling vocabulary."

As you develop your feeling vocabulary, the next step in great parenting is to learn to answer emotion with emotion. Here are some examples of what this looks and sounds like.

- "I can see that you're hurting (or sad, or scared, or __________). It saddens me that you feel so alone at school."

- "I can see how disappointed you are that you weren't invited to the party. I know that's disappointing to you."
- "I can appreciate that you're upset about missing the game. I know that's disappointing to you."
- "I know you're really frustrated right now because you're having trouble understanding algebra. I want you to know that I care about you and will help you in any way I can."
- "I know you're anxious about this big exam. I want you to know I'll be praying for you. I love you!"
- "I'm committed to going through this with you."
- "Can you share with me how I've hurt you, and how it made you feel? I want to understand and make it right."
- "I see that I hurt you by my ____________, and that was wrong of me. Will you forgive me?"

As you allow your heart to feel what your head knows and then communicate that to your child, you become a channel of comfort and blessing—and that's great parenting. Ephesians 4:29 actually speaks of ministering God's grace as we share words that encourage and build up. Language is a powerful gift from God. It allows us to worship God, communicate information with one another, and fully express emotions. Proverbs speaks to the power and impact of our words and their power to heal.

- A soothing tongue is a tree of life, but a perversion in it crushes the spirit. (Prov. 15:4 NASB)
- Death and life are in the power of the tongue. (Prov. 18:21 NASB)

- Pleasant words are a honeycomb, sweet to the soul and healing to the bones. (Prov. 16:24 NASB)
- Anxiety in a man's heart weighs it down, but a good word makes it glad. (Prov. 12:25 NASB)[8]

A mother at a seminar revealed how she's able to encourage her quiet daughter to open up and share her personal feelings. As the mother is helping her daughter get ready for bed, one will say to the other, "High-Low?" And that's the signal for the other to share the high points of her day and then the low points.[9] It's a fun and effective way to encourage someone to share.

A child who is emotionally intelligent is able to recognize a feeling when it happens. He's not victimized by his feelings. He's able to stop the intensity of his emotion and enforce his own standards. He's also able to predict what sets him off, avoid or minimize those things, and learn effective coping skills.

This is also a more stress-resistant child, one who can handle the ups and downs and upsets of life. Because of understanding his own emotions, he is able to understand the emotions and responses of others. This child tends to motivate himself more as well as get along better with others. This is a responsible child, and I think this is what most of us as parents want for our children.

The good news is, it's possible with your guidance.

10

Secret 10

Great Parents Avoid These Ten Steps to Disaster

Admit it—your child has been known to make unreasonable demands, and you've been known to give in.

Don't worry. We've all done it. One of the reasons parents cave in to their children's requests is that they become weary. What they do to get through to their children or to motivate them doesn't work. So to get rid of the hassle, they throw in the towel.

There are ten things that all of us (yes, all of us) have done at one time or another that contribute to this problem. Some parents make this their pattern even though it's not effective. And these just give the child more and more control. That's the bad news. The good news is that great parents know *all* of these approaches can be changed.

What are those ten disastrous approaches? Let's identify them one by one.

UNCLEAR REQUESTS

First, we give unclear requests or directions. What may be obvious to us isn't necessarily clear to our children. We're either vague, tentative, say too much, or put it in language our children don't understand. Have you ever been on the receiving end of requests or directions like these? If so, did you feel like complying? Probably not. And neither will your child. "Don't eat too much" or "Don't stay out too late" or "Don't play too rough." What do these requests mean? When you call your child on any of these infractions you'll get an argument. His idea of what is too much is different than yours. Spell it out from the beginning and you'll avoid a lot of conflict.

When you make a request, make it clear and simple, and focus on the child's behavior, not his or her character. General, vague comments like these are not enforceable: "Do a good job on the lawn" or "Get home at a reasonable time" or "Don't stay out too late." Try these instead: "Dinner is at 5:30. Please be here by 5:15 to help" or "When you clean your room, put all dirty clothes in the hamper, all clean ones on hangers, and dust the furniture." These give your child a specific message of what you expect.

REPEATING OURSELVES

Second, we repeat ourselves. If you need to say something twice (or three times, or five) you probably were being ignored. Now, that's not a pleasant experience. So when we repeat, we tend to use the same words, but intensify the presentation a bit. But if what you said the first time didn't register, why would you believe it will the second time? If something needs repeating, it needs to be repackaged. Get your child's attention by going where your child is (no talking from room to room); put your hand gently on his shoulder; speak softly and slowly, and you will likely be heard. Remember, children (especially boys) have difficulty doing more than one thing at a time. It's vital that they stop what they're doing in order for your message to connect.

When I give a command softly to my golden retrievers, I usually get an immediate response. They know the tone I'm using means they need to respond.

REMINDING

Reminding is another game parents hate to play and rightly so. Every time we remind someone, we feed our own irritation. It takes energy, and the older the child, the more irritation we experience. "Why can't that child remember anything I say?" It's a way the child gets us to take responsibility for something that rightfully belongs to her. And when a child forgets to take her lunch to school and we rush in to bail her out, we feel more of an urgency to remind her the next time and the child has less of a reason to remember.

OPTIONAL OBEDIENCE

Sometimes the reason our children don't respond is because they know we don't mean what we say. They know "right now" means it can happen anytime. They know "not until you've done your chores" means it's all right to do it now, chores can wait. And the worst one is when they know that our "no" means "yes" or "maybe"! When your child believes that complying with your request is optional, it shows that your limits are not clear or strong enough, and that they have not been enforced in the past.

Have you ever told your child to turn the radio or TV or computer off and heard, "Yeah, I will" or "In a minute"? Those responses usually mean just the opposite, and when you remind them, you usually get the same response. It doesn't have to be that way. There are many children who learn to respond to the first request. They learned early on that noncompliance meant consequences. They learned they could depend upon their parents to do what they said they would do. What have those parents done? They have made eye contact with their children, made the request clear and concise, asked their children to repeat what was said, and gave directions according to the children's ability to remember.

Every child is wired or created in a unique way. Some have the ability to remember more for a long period of time. Others forget on the way to their room half of what was said. These latter children need small pieces of information. They can handle only small doses. Some children can retain for hours and others just for minutes.[1]

Some parents (if their children are old enough to read) give them instructions in writing since so many children are visual learners. This can work well with boys especially.

By the way, most children have a very effective weapon to use when we repeat or remind. They have a little switch that tunes us out.

REASONING

When repeating and reminding don't work, we fall back on reasoning. "I always thought if my child knew the reasons for what I asked, she would be more cooperative." Our reasons make sense to us, but may not to our children. All the reasons in the world may not help if your child doesn't want to cooperate. Yes, it's true, we do give reasons to begin with so our children learn. But after that you don't need to go over them again and again. It's like an appeal but it doesn't help. Responding to those "why" questions isn't necessary if you clearly explained it once. It's a stall tactic and an expression of resistance and it could be we are over-explaining to our children. Not every "why" question needs or deserves an explanation. Some parents have listed the reasons in writing if their children are old enough. Others have told their children to take a time out and think back to what the reasons were when they explained them.

> When someone is trying to persuade you to change your mind or purchase something or do something, all you have to do is employ the broken record technique and you'll win.

One parent said, "Oh, it was so exasperating. My son would ask 'Why?' and I would explain and he would say it again. The message I was getting was my answer wasn't good enough for him." Continual questioning or arguments are a message, "Your reasons aren't good enough for me."

Bargaining

There's another response that a child just loves to engage you in—bargaining. There are some cultures where you never pay the initial price quoted to you—it would be an insult to do so. Some children must think they're part of that culture! They constantly try to bargain with you. If a child persists, pleads, whines, and digs in his heels, and you begin to waiver, concede, and finally bend, the child learns a lesson. He can win. And he's on the way not only to being indulged now, but to getting his way the rest of his life. He learns to argue, and sometimes these encounters turn ugly and become quarrels. Scripture has something to say about this:

> People without good sense find fault with their neighbors, but those with understanding keep quiet. (Prov. 11:12 NCV)

> Starting a quarrel is like a leak in a dam, so stop it before a fight breaks out. (Prov. 17:14 NCV)

> Foolish people are always fighting, but avoiding quarrels will bring you honor. (Prov. 20:3 NCV)

> If it is possible, as far as it depends on you, live at peace with everyone. (Rom. 12:18)

> Get rid of all bitterness, rage and anger, brawling and slander, along with every form of malice. (Eph. 4:31)

How do you stay out of quarrels and bargaining? How do you stay out of getting worn down? Years ago I learned an approach called the Broken Record Technique. When someone is trying to persuade you to change your mind or purchase something or do something, all you have to do is employ the broken record technique and you'll win. Most people can't last against this defense. If someone is pressuring you to buy something and trying to find out the reason why you won't buy it (which you don't have to give and shouldn't give!) all you have to say to whatever they say is, "No, thank you. I'm just not interested," again and again and again, and the other person will give up. If a friend is pressuring you to attend something and you don't want to go, all you have to say is, "Thank you for asking, but I'm unable to attend." Again, you don't have to give your reason.

Let's say you've asked your son to clean his room before he goes over to his friend's place to go swimming. He agreed, but he hasn't done it yet. Jimmy runs by and says, "See ya, Mom. I'm going over to Ken's to swim."

Mom: "Wait up, Jimmy. You said earlier that you would clean your room before you went to Ken's."

Jimmy: "But Mom, I need to leave now. It would take too long to clean it."

Mom: "That may be the case, Jimmy, and feel free to go when your room is clean."

Jimmy: "Mom—Ken called and wants to show me stuff before the others get there."

Mom: "I'm sure he did, and feel free to go as soon as your room is clean."

Jimmy: "Why can't I do it later? Other kids get to play first and then they do the work. It's not fair."

Mom: "That may be true, Jimmy, and feel free to go after your room is clean."[2]

Jimmy cleaned his room. Mom didn't go ballistic, raise her voice, or get angry. She simply used a quiet, controlled, persistent, determined statement that deflected every onslaught Jimmy sent her way. And you can do the same thing. Can you think of phrases you could use? Write out some of the statements your child uses on you and practice your response in advance. Use phrases like "feel free to ..." or "You're welcome to go when ..."

You're not threatening or badgering or bargaining. You're calling your child back to your request and/or his agreement. You're simply helping him learn to follow through and become trustworthy. You can also use statements like "We've talked about this enough. Please don't bring it up again. If you do ..." or "It's time for action. You can do what I asked or ... Which do you choose?"

LECTURING

There's another approach parents use quite frequently and to their detriment—lecturing. And this word is not being used here in a positive sense. It's when we try to correct a child by teaching, giving all the facts, often pointing out what she's been doing wrong, questioning whether her brain was in gear or not, all the time hoping that this approach will solve the problem once and for all. It's called "tell them, teach them, and they'll shape up." Well, for a student to learn something she has to listen, want to learn, be open to change, and excited about discovering something new. I don't think this is the position of most children when they're being lectured to. They're usually waiting out the tirade until you're through.

There's a principle great parents have learned to follow. If they want to be heard by their children more, they talk less. The greater the amount of verbiage that comes from us, the more it closes a child's ears and mouth. There's a malady that hits children when we begin to lecture. It's called PLG—this stands for Parent Lecture Gaze. Our children's eyes begin to gloss over when we start in, and even more so if they know it's lecture #17. Oh, they may grunt every four or five minutes just to let us know they're awake but that's nothing more than a reflex. Kids see a lecture as a long monologue sprinkled with phrases like "Now, see here" or "You need to listen, young man" or "and furthermore...."

Parents tell me time and time again they have trouble getting their children to listen. I tell them to try the following:

1. Be sure you get your child's attention. He needs to listen to you with his eyes since non-verbal communication accounts for 5 percent of a message.
2. If your child is a boy, remember he doesn't hear as well as a girl, so you may need to speak a bit more loudly.
3. Don't give a big answer to your child's little question.
4. Use the "One word rule." That's right, say one word and no more. If your child comes and drops his coat on the floor or chair, instead of going on with "How many times have I told you …" and being tuned out, just say, "Coat." If your daughter forgets to turn out the lights just say, "Lights." Save your words and you'll have better responses.[3]

A lecture is an example of the law of diminishing returns—the more said, the less heard. And remember, the older a child the more the definition of a lecture changes. To a teen, it's probably any input over ten words![4]

There's something else to consider. When you lecture, going over and over what the problem is, you tend to reinforce the behavior and heighten the probability that it will arise again. A lecture doesn't solve the problem. Going back to our example, you could lecture Jimmy about his room and keeping his word until you're blue in the face, and he would still argue with you. But if you ask him, "Jimmy, what was the original agreement?" no matter what tactic he takes to avoid answering, keep repeating the question in a calm voice, and you will eventually make progress. If you get the classic response, "I don't know," just say, "When you remember, then we can continue our conversation and the day's activities. Let me know when you remember." Sooner or later, he will realize that the only way to get to his friend's house is to answer your question, which implies action.

If your child is an introvert, be sure to say, "Take some time to think about it." Remember, an introvert child has to think in the privacy of his own mind before he can speak. You won't get any response if you put pressure on him. It's not a defect, it's just the way he was created.

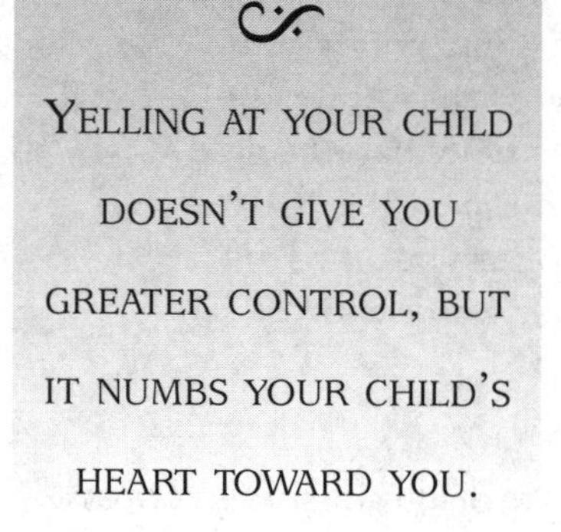

Instead of lecturing and going over what your child did wrong, talk about what you would like him to do differently the next time, and you are more likely to see a change. Point toward the desired behavior, making that the last message your child hears—that's the one he'll remember.

When your child does follow your instructions, let him know you appreciate this step: "I really like it when you choose to follow directions the first time." When you say this, you've sent a message that you believe your child is capable of doing what you ask.[5]

LAST RESORT APPROACH

Another trap we fall into is the "Last Resort" approach. These are not pretty techniques for a parent to employ. Pleading or cajoling shows that we've lost most of the battle. Another word for plead is beg. When a parent begs a child, what kind of message is that sending? Does it generate respect in the child for the parent? Not usually. Cajole means to coax with flattery and insincere talk or to wheedle. It's another word for manipulate.

And when these don't work, it's just a short walk down the road to manipulating by silence or shame.

Yelling

Surely every parent has also stooped to raising his or her voice or yelling. Have you ever been yelled at? If so, how did you feel? Did you remember what you were supposed to? Did you want to follow through with what was expected from you, or did you feel more like digging in your heels? Did you want a better or closer relationship with this person? "No" is probably the answer to most of these questions. And this is probably how a child feels when a parent raises his voice or yells at him. It also shows that the parent has lost control. If your face gets red and veins pop out and you're on the verge of hysteria, your children are probably enjoying the show.

Yelling at your child doesn't give you greater control, but it numbs your child's heart toward you. He is less willing to listen and cooperate. As you push up the volume, a child's ability to hear diminishes.

If your child does respond, it's usually out of fear and intimidation. Very little lasting learning occurs. I don't know many parents who are proud to say, "My child is afraid of me."

Threats and Fear

When nothing else works, we sometimes rely on threatening. The "or else" statements become a big part of your vocabulary. Threats can generate fear and compliance, or they can promote defiance: "Go ahead, see if I care." It's a great way to feed a power struggle and cause more distance in the parent-child relationship.

When you command your child to do something, it's like waving a red cape in front of a bull. It's a call to battle. You end up feeling more like adversaries than allies.[6]

All of us as parents have become desperate at one time or another—when our children aren't complying or are acting out in public or it's dinnertime or the end of an exhausting day and we're at our wit's end. That's when we reach into our bag of "Parental Last Resorts!" for a solution. Many of these are based on fear. We say things like the following:

- "Put your toys away this minute, or else!" And we think this will work since our children are afraid of being punished. (What does "or else" mean to your child?)
- "If you act like that, I don't want you around. You'll get sent to your room." Could it be our children respond because they're afraid of losing our love?
- "If your room isn't clean when I'm ready to go, I'll just have to leave you." The fear of abandonment works on some, but others never hear you.
- "If you do what I say right now, we'll stop at McDonald's on the way home," or "If you don't rake the leaves, you can forget the soccer game today." Some children respond to threats or promises because they're afraid of missing out.

A parent told me she didn't use fear. She used questions and reasoning. It sounded good to me so I asked a couple of questions, "What do you say?"

She said, "If the kids aren't getting along I just say, 'Why did you hit your brother? Was it loving? Was it? What if someone hit you in the back?'" (I wonder how a child feels with these questions.)

I asked, "How do you reason with them?"

"Oh, I say, 'Now, you two talk to each other. You can work it out, can't you? It's better if you do rather than me. You know what I'll do.'"

My last question was, "How old are your children?"

"Oh, they're four and six."

How many adults can answer "why" questions? I wonder whether her children felt OK about themselves after these questions. I wonder if these two knew how to work it out at that age. Even if they had been ten and twelve, unless they had been taught to solve problems, they couldn't work it out on their own.

Here are some statements that won't work.

- I told you not to do it again. How many times do I have to tell you? (Do you really want to know?)
- Jimmy, you had better stop it. You're going to be sorry.
- Wait until I get home. You're going to catch it then.
- I didn't think you were this type of child. How could you?
- Wouldn't you like to behave for me today?
- Please, won't you do me a favor and cooperate?
- You'd better shape up.
- Would you like it if I did that to you?
- That's enough for today.

Put yourself in a small child's place. What do these statements mean? Does she understand all of the words? If she takes everything literally, what messages does she come away with? Will she be motivated to change?

Keep in mind that your child can't think abstractly as well as an adult. In addition, remember that all children change when they're under pressure. They become younger emotionally. They regress, and the greater the pressure, the more the regression. Children bounce back and forth emotionally. This is normal. So when they're upset and we tell them "Act your age" or "Don't be such a baby" or "Grow up," in a sense, we're asking them to do the impossible.

Because we're larger (and often louder), it's easy to intimidate children and use fear as a means of control. Fear may control for a while, but it doesn't teach, and it doesn't change lives. It doesn't build up, it doesn't bring lasting results, and it won't solve your problem with your child. It won't develop a better relationship between you and your child.

YOUR CHILD WILL BE INCONSISTENT. YOUR CHILD WILL MAKE MISTAKES. YOUR CHILD WILL NOT DO THINGS EXACTLY THE WAY YOU WANT. WHY? SIMPLE. HE'S A CHILD.

Using any kind of fear response actually brings about the opposite of what you want to happen in your child. It limits his or her ability to learn from you. Some parents will disagree and say, "It works. He conforms."

But fear creates stress in a child. Stress releases hormones, and one of the chemicals it releases, cortisol, actually interferes with memory and learning. When you control your child by fear, you can short circuit the brain, and you hear those phrases you just love to hear when you're trying to get something across to your child: "I don't know" or "I don't remember." (And if your child is introverted in his personality and has to think in the privacy of his mind before speaking, the more pressure you put on him, the less you will hear. This is why it's so important to adapt your questions and responses to the uniqueness of each child).

When your child gives these responses under stress, they're true! They don't remember well. They can't. This is the way

God created us to respond under pressure. Fear responses don't work. They bring about what you don't want. They don't focus on what you would like to be different, but instead on what was done wrong.

How do you know if you're using a fear-based response? Sometimes the thoughts or questions in our minds give the clue. Have you ever asked, "How do I get my child to …?" or "How can I make my child …?" Of course. We all have, but what do these questions imply? Control. And we do want her to be under some control. But what would happen if your question was, "How can I help my child be more likely to choose …?" That's teaching. That's helping a child for the future when you're not around.

As parents, we are constantly sending messages to our children. But there are two important questions to ask ourselves: What are we trying to communicate, and what is the effect of our words upon our children?

Most of us have spouted the following:

> "What's wrong with you?"
> "I warned you, didn't I?"
> "I told you before!"
> "You know better than that."
> "You should have known."
> "You just don't listen."
> "How could you have forgotten?"

What do all these messages say to a child? Basically, you blew it, you messed up, you're not performing the way I want you to, you're not trying hard enough. Will these messages bring about what you want, or are they a vent for parental frustration? Parents are not perfect, and children are less than perfect. When we make statements like these, could it be we think, "You know, my child is doing this on purpose, just to upset me. I bet he woke up this morning and plotted how he could mess up and disrupt my life." Most of us wouldn't go down that road of thought, but sometimes what we say might sound that way.

Your child will be inconsistent. Your child will make mistakes. Your child will not do things exactly the way you want. Why? Simple. He's a child, and he learns by trial and error. So encourage his efforts, look for progress to praise, and help him learn from failure.[7]

When you try to "get" or "make" your child do something, you end up on a slippery slope. You might cajole, coerce, bribe, beg, force, threaten, give up, and then as a last resort give in.[8] The final outcome has led to indulgence, and this is probably the last thing you ever wanted for your child. (Take out your dictionary, and write out the definitions that you find for each of those eight words. Read them over each morning. It could help you not use them.)

Instead, talk with your child. Point out what you want, and believe that they will (eventually) do it.

Unfortunately, some parents have swung too far in getting rid of fear-based techniques and ended up spoiling their children. Giving up ineffective techniques will work only if you replace them with something that is more effective. Children need the support and stability of a secure, stable, "gently" firm parent.

11

Secret 11

Great Parents Learn to Be Limit-Setters

A young parent sat in my office, a confused expression on her face. "I just don't know what to do with my two children. I seem to get such conflicting advice from everyone. I have one set of friends who tell me to be strict and set these firm limits. Don't let the children argue. They just have to do what I say whether they like it or not. Don't give in. The problem is I take a look at their kids and it hasn't worked with them. Maybe they don't practice what they're preaching.

"Another set of friends tells me to be a loving parent. I need to be a giving parent. My life needs to revolve around my children and give them every possible opportunity. After all, they're only children for a little while. But I don't like what I see in their kids. They're like little dictators ruling the house—and talk about attitude!

"So I vacillate between setting limits and giving in—I really question whether or not I'm being a good parent. And I think my children know I'm uncertain and work it to their advantage. I even end up questioning what my role is at times, and finally there are days when I've had it. I'm worn out. I don't have any more to give."

This parent isn't alone. Many end up feeling this way. What about you?

PARENTAL BURNOUT

Have you ever felt worn down, worn out, and weary from hassling with your child? Who hasn't? If you find yourself this way it could mean your own resources are low. Some parents suffer from parental burnout! How could this happen? It's easy. All you have to do is give and give and give and never replenish yourself. It doesn't take much for this to happen. And it's even worse when you're not appreciated or when what you try to do doesn't work. If you don't give yourself any time to recuperate, it will happen. And if you don't have other people in your life who can support you ... well, isolation is a dangerous road.

How can you give if your well is empty? There is an area in Southern California called Death Valley. It's hot, desolate, and arid. It's not really a fun place to visit. But centuries ago it wasn't like this. It was a large lake with a river flowing into and out of it. Over time the river flowing in got smaller and smaller and eventually dried up. But the river flowing out continued to take water out of the lake until there was no more water to drain. It dried up. Parents dry up as well. They give and give without taking in and soon their well is dry.

A great parent knows that it's all right to take care of yourself. It's all right to get some rest and ask others to help. It's not a sign of being a loving parent to give without receiving or replenishing. You're not neglecting your child by taking a break. You're more likely to neglect him by not taking a break. Perhaps it would help you to post the following quote from *Boundaries with Kids:* "Remember that parenting is a temporary job, not an identity." Kids with great parents who have a life learn both that they aren't the center of the universe and that they can be free to pursue their own dreams.[1]

Another reason you may feel worn out is that you've taught your child something you never intended to teach him. Many parents fall into this trap—they train their children to know how far to push before Mom or Dad will give in. Each time you give after initially saying no, your child files the event away in his memory bank. With each incident he gains strength, determination, and tenacity. With each parent-child encounter he is able to dig his heels in and engage you in a stronger power struggle. As one parent said, "The trick of parenting is to hold on to your limit one more time than your children hold on to the demand. That's all you need—one more."[2]

When you stand firm, stubborn, and embedded in rock, you send a message to your child: "It just won't work, so give up"—and they begin to back down.[3]

Perhaps we need to be reminded from time to time of what our role is as a parent.

Functions of the Parenting Role

The authors of *Boundaries with Kids* suggest that the parenting role consists of several main functions. Scripture states that children are "under guardians and managers" until the appropriate time (Gal. 4:2 NASB). We'll look at the role of guardian first.

As a parent, you are legally responsible for your child. You also have to provide, protect, and preserve. A child doesn't have the wisdom or ability to protect himself. What child knows right from wrong, dangerous from safe, or good from better? None. They're not concerned about consequences but want immediate gratification.

How do you get wisdom? You get it from what a child doesn't have—experience. Your job is to provide the right amount of freedom, not too much or too little, so that your child learns.

The Book of Proverbs has something to say about this:

> Listen, my sons, to a father's instruction;
> pay attention and gain understanding.
> I give you sound learning,
> so do not forsake my teaching.
> When I was a boy in my father's house,
> still tender, and an only child of my mother,
> he taught me and said,
> "Lay hold of my words with all your heart;
> keep my commands and you will live.
> Get wisdom, get understanding;
> do not forget my words
> or swerve from them." (Prov. 4:1–5)

In *The 3000 Year-Old Guide to Parenting,* Wes Haystead says that the words *understanding*, *knowledge*, and *wisdom* keep recurring throughout Proverbs. These terms refer to the ability to think clearly, to connect facts and experiences, and to come to a responsible judgment as a result. They describe the capacity to learn and to apply that learning to life's situations.

While these verses strongly advocate obedience to parental commands—"do not forsake … keep my commands … do not forget my words or swerve from them"—a broader intent is clearly evident. The goal reaches beyond producing children who do what they are told. The objective is to equip them to think wisely—"Get wisdom, get understanding"—and to make personal commitments to do what is right—"Lay hold of my words with all your heart."

A good math teacher is not satisfied when students can compute the right answer. The teacher also wants each student to be able to explain how the problem was solved and why that was the proper approach to the solution.

In life, even more than in math, Proverbs recognizes that children need to be taken beyond repeating learned answers. They need to be equipped to discern what is best in new situations.

The normal, active children in our neighborhood have compiled over the years a notable list of not-too-bright escapades, activities that caused adults to respond profoundly with "You should have known better than to ...!" Among their dubious exploits have been a range of fairly typical, childlike behaviors that include

- ruining perfectly good shoes by sloshing in mud puddles, an action perhaps understandable when committed by Southern California youngsters unfamiliar with rain;
- getting stuck inside a drainage pipe, requiring a fire department rescue;
- having an olive fight in the kitchen at 4:00 a.m. during a sleepover birthday party;
- putting a can of soda in the freezer, then forgetting it (don't try this at home, folks!);
- cutting hunks of hair from one's own head or that of a willing victim;
- setting fire to weeds in the backyard, requiring another visit from the fire department;
- ruining a kitchen pan and burning a hole in a stove by letting hot chocolate boil dry;

- puncturing a soccer ball by kicking it into a rose bush;
- losing an assortment of jackets, sweaters, sweatshirts, caps, baseball gloves, soccer balls, and similar apparel at school, parks, church, friends' houses, and various unknown locations.

Any neighborhood with children could compile a similar list of childhood escapades. We expect children, being immature, to do foolish things on occasion.[4]

Now let's look at the role of manager. This is someone who sees that things get done. You provide the "self-discipline" your child doesn't have so he follows through and learns. How do you do this? You control resources, teach, set limits (there's that key phrase again), require your child to take ownership for a problem and responsibility for the consequences. You correct, discipline, and help your child build skills.[5]

As a rule children don't know what they are doing. They have little idea how to handle life so that it works right. That's why God gave them parents—to love them, give them structure, and guide them into maturity. Basically, children will mature to the level the parent structures them, and no higher. The parent's limitations in being able to be responsible and teach responsibility influence how well children learn responsibility. Children don't have it in them to grow themselves up. They respond and adapt to how they are parented.[6]

Setting limits isn't about being authoritarian or more powerful than a child. It's not like being a drill sergeant barking out orders left and right. Setting limits with children has nothing to do with volume, intensity, or how definite you are.

Setting limits is about being a great parent by being lovingly assertive. When you hear the word *assertive*, what comes to mind? Is it a negative or positive image? It's a better option than being passive or aggressive. Being assertive is making sure you are heard and understood. It can be firm but kind, strong but gentle. It is better soft than loud and with a smile rather than a frown. If you want something, say you want it.

Setting limits involves asking the child questions, offering choices, inviting positive responses, and using consequences. These are responses that teach children how to make decisions, force responsibility, and avoid being indulged. It's better if they learn to make decisions, for the lesson stays with them. When we tell or order them to do something we may have compliance, but did they learn?

> ONE OF THE BEST WAYS FOR A CHILD TO LEARN TO BE INSECURE IS FOR HIM TO REALIZE HE HAS MORE POWER THAN HIS PARENTS.

Consider the difference in each of these examples:

- A child smarts off to his mom. She could say, "Don't you talk to me in that way!" or she could say, "I can hear you're upset in your tone of voice. I'll be glad to listen to you when your voice is soft like mine."
- A child is putting off his chores. His dad could say, "Hurry up and get those chores done now," or he could say, "Feel free to join us for some games when your chores are done."
- A brother and sister are arguing and pulling on a toy. Their mom could say, "Stop it, you two. Try to get along, can't you?" or she could say, "You two can join the rest of us when you've worked it out."
- A daughter stays on the phone instead of picking up her room. Her mom could say, "Get off the phone now and get your room in shape," or she could say, "I'll take you shopping when

> your room is picked up according to the posted agreement."[7]

Children as well as adults need clear limits in their lives. For security, children want to know what's expected, where they stand with others, how far to go, and what to expect if they go over that line. If there are no limits, children don't know how to behave acceptably. If they're raised without these, watch out! Their lives will be filled with upset, rejection, disapproval, and perhaps not fitting in.

When you set limits, you're teaching your child as well as avoiding indulging them.

Have you ever thought of your child as a researcher? He's doing this constantly by testing, exploring, gathering information, observing, and figuring out cause-and-effect relationships that are all used to make decisions about life.

I've done a lot of hiking in the Grand Teton National Park. Some of the hikes were enjoyable because I knew where I was going; the trail markers were clear and accurate. I've also gotten lost on some hikes when the markers were gone or inaccurate or never existed in the first place. I was confused. And so are children when their markers in life are gone or confusing. Limits tell them "Here is the acceptable path and here is the unacceptable one."

Limits teach the child who's in control. Every child has power and control, but she doesn't know how much until she starts pushing. If she's been given too much, she invades the adult world, roaming around where she has no business being. A child is just like a new puppy brought into a family. She thinks the whole world is hers and she's the top dog. But in time she learns who's in charge and which rooms she can and cannot go into. The boundaries have been set.

One of the best ways for a child to learn to be insecure is for him to realize he has more power than his parents. Limits show a child what he can handle on his own and what he cannot. They also make him feel safe. He needs parents he can count on to be there, to say what is right or wrong, acceptable or unacceptable, and to show him they have more power than he does. It's the parent who must have parent power.[8]

Are children going to like limits? Of course not. Are they going to push against them and try to get you to change? Of course. Your child is going to protest. We have a nation of protesters. Groups gather together to protest against court decisions. People protest the cutting down of trees by going up a tree and sitting there for a month. Workers protest against their employers by walking in circles and carrying placards.

Let your children protest, but don't change the limit, and don't get caught up in the protest. Dr. Cloud and Dr. Townsend give a good example of getting caught up versus sticking to the limit.

Scenario One

> "No, Kathy, you can't go to the movies today."
>
> "That's not fair! Marcia's going. I hate your stupid rules."
>
> "Kathy, that's a bad attitude. After all the things I have let you do, the least you could do is stop arguing with me."
>
> "It isn't fair! All the other kids get to go. Michael gets to go more than me."
>
> "I let you go to lots of things this week. Don't give me all that stuff about I don't let you do anything. Don't you remember when you went the other day?"
>
> "But I want to go today. You don't even care!"
>
> "I do care. How could you say that? All I ever do is cart you around from one place to another. How can you say I don't care? Now straighten up

your attitude, or you aren't going anywhere for a week!"

Scenario Two

"No, Kathy, you can't go to the movies today. You have to do your chores first."

"That's not fair! Marcia's going. I hate your stupid rules."

"I know. It's frustrating when you don't get to go to the movies again."

"But I want to go today. You don't even care!'

"I know you're frustrated and angry. It's tough to have to work before you have fun. I feel that way too."

"I hate living here! I don't ever get to do anything."

"I know. It's hard to miss the movies when you really want to go."

"Well, if you know so much, then let me go."

"I know you want to. It's tough. But no."

"But if I miss this one, there won't be another sneak preview this summer."

"That's sad. It's a long time till next summer. I can see why you hate missing it so much."

Finally the child gets bored with not getting anywhere, either with moving the limit or frustrating the parent, and she gives up. She must accept reality.[9]

Here's an example of eleven-year-old Billy's disrespect of his mom's limits:

"Mom, I'm going down to Joey's to play hockey. See ya later."

"No, Billy. You can't go. It's time to do your homework."

"Come on, Mom! Everyone's going. I can do my homework later."

"Billy, I understand you want to go, but we agreed that if you went swimming, you would work on your homework before dinner."

"Yeah, but I could do it after dinner."

"An agreement is an agreement. I don't want to talk about it anymore."

"You're just stupid. You don't understand anything. You're a big, fat, stupid."

If this sounds familiar, don't fret. Normal children naturally hate limits when you first set them. Your test is what are you going to do when the child expresses disrespect. It is normal for disrespect to occur, but it is not normal for it to continue. The cure is empathy and correction, then consequences.

EMPATHY AND CORRECTION

- "Billy, I understand that you're really disappointed, but that's not the way to talk to me. Calling me 'stupid' is not okay. It hurts my feelings. It is okay to be sad or mad, but I won't allow name calling."
- "Billy, I understand that you're upset. But when you call me stupid, how do you think that makes me feel?" (Wait for an answer so he has to think about how another person feels.) "How do you feel when people call you names? Would you like to be treated that way?"
- "Billy, I hear that you're ticked, and when you talk to me more respectfully, I'll be glad to listen. I won't listen to people who call me stupid. If you are upset about something, tell me in a different way."

- "Billy, please think about what you just said and say it better."[10]

In the book *Setting Limits* by Robert MacKenzie a cool-down technique is suggested. It's an excellent way to interrupt anger, keep it from escalating, and regain self-control.

It may not always be easy to do, especially if your emotions have begun to rise, but with preplanning, application of Scripture, prayer, and practice it will work. Memorizing and posting the following Scripture will help it come more easily:

> But now put away and rid yourselves [completely] of all these things: anger, rage, bad feeling toward others, curses and slander, and foulmouthed abuse and shameful utterances from your lips! (Col. 3:8 AB)

Scripture also teaches us not to provoke others to anger:

> The terror of a king is as the roaring of a lion; whoever provokes him to anger or angers himself against him sins against his own life. (Prov. 20:2 AB)

The Bible directs us to be "slow to anger" (that is, to control our anger) and to be careful of close association with others who are constantly angry or hostile:

> A hot-tempered man stirs up strife, but the slow to anger calms a dispute. (Prov. 15:18 NASB)

> He who is slow to anger is better than the mighty, he who rules his [own] spirit than he who takes a city. (Prov. 16:32 AB)

> Make no friendships with a man given to anger, and a wrathful man do not associate, lest you learn his ways and get yourself into a snare. (Prov. 22:24–25 AB)

Scripture also speaks of justified anger. An example is found in the life of the Lord Jesus:

> And He glanced around at them with vexation and anger, grieved at the hardening of their hearts, and said to the man, "Hold out your hand." He held it out, and his hand was [completely] restored. (Mark 3:5 AB)

SETTING LIMITS INVOLVES GIVING CHOICES. THE PARENT WHO GIVES HIS CHILD CHOICES WILL HAVE A CHILD WHO IS BEING GROOMED TO BE AN ADULT.

In Ephesians 4:26 the apostle Paul speaks of two kinds of anger and how to deal with both:

> When angry, do not sin; do not ever let your wrath (your exasperation, your fury or indignation) last until the sun goes down. (AB)

There are three ways to implement this approach with your child. If you're both upset, you could say, "It seems like we both need to calm down. Let's take a five-minute breather. I'll meet you in your room and let's both think about how we could talk to one another in a different way." Be sure to use a timer.

If only your child is angry you could say, "I can see you're angry. Let's take a five-minute time-out to cool down. You can be in your room or the living room. Which one do you choose?"

If you are the one getting angry you could say, "I'm angry right now and I don't want to be. I want to calm down. I'll be in the other room for a while and when I'm calm we'll talk."[11]

CHOICES

Setting limits involves giving choices. That's realistic, because life is full of choices. Some just happen, while others are created. The parent who gives his child choices will have a child who is being groomed to be an adult. A child who is not forced to make choices will have more difficulty coping with life. When you give your child choices, you activate his brain and also make it easier on yourself. I've talked with parents of three-year-olds, six-year-olds, and nine-year-olds who all had the same question: "How can we have fewer hassles with the kids? What I ask them to do is simple, everyday stuff. There's got to be a better way to make a simple request, isn't there?"

There is. The authors of *Parenting with Love and Logic* have a very workable suggestion—use "thinking words."

Children learn better from what they tell themselves than from what we tell them. They may do what we order them to do, but then their motivation for obedience comes from a voice other than their own—ours. Kids believe something that comes from inside their own heads. When they choose an option, they do the thinking, they make the choice, and the lesson sticks with them. That's why from early childhood on, great parents must always be asking thinking-word questions: "Would you rather carry your coat or wear it?" "Would you rather put your boots on now or in the car?" "Would you rather play nicely in front of the television or be noisy in your room?"

We don't use fighting words: "You put that coat on now!" "Because I said put your boots on, that's why! It's snowing outside." "I'm trying to watch this football game. So be quiet!"[12]

Do you see the difference? Offering choices encourages cooperation without argument or hassle.

The authors also make this suggestion: Instead of telling your children what to do, what you won't allow, or what you won't do for them, state the opposite.

Tell your child what you will allow—"Feel free to join us for dinner as soon as you've finished your chores."

Tell your child what you will do—"I'll be glad to help you with your homework as soon as you've cleared the table and rinsed everything."

Tell your child what you will provide—"You can eat what we're having or you can see if you like the next meal better."[13]

Can you do this? Of course you can, with practice. Think of an incident (or several) that you wish had gone better. Write them down the way you remember them going. Now rewrite them, giving your child a choice. Remember some of the phrases that have been suggested: "Feel free," "I'll be glad," and "You may."

Yes, it will take some thought on your part.

Yes, it will take some time on your part.

And yes, this may surprise your child so that he or she begins to think and comply. What do you have to lose by trying something different?

Whenever you have rules, you need consequences. They are the second part of setting limits. They let a child know what is acceptable and what isn't—and most important, who's in charge. They also hold a child responsible for his choices and behavior.

CONSEQUENCES

Consequences are good training for adulthood. When you don't pay your phone bill, your service is cut off, and the same goes for electricity and gas. If you fail to pay your credit card bill, just wait until you try to use it again.

I've been using these principles for almost forty years. I first learned about them from Dr. Randolph Dreikur's writings, *Children, the Challenge*, and from one of my graduate school professors who had studied under him. I discovered these principles worked with one child or one hundred fifty children.

For a time I was a youth pastor, and for some meetings at church we would have over one hundred teenagers. When we had a special speaker, I wanted the kids to hear the message, and I didn't want a lot of disruptions. So I used a simple rule. I would say, "We're glad you're here tonight to hear our speaker. I'd like you to get the most out of what he has to say, and I know you would too, since you chose to be here. I have one simple rule we'll be following. All I ask is that you give him your undivided attention and listen without disrupting anyone around you. And when you do that you've chosen to stay. If you choose to make noise and disturb others around you, you choose to leave the meeting. Thanks for your cooperation."

I'd wait for the one who would push the limit to see if I meant it, and when that happened, he or she was asked to leave. The teen wasn't kicked out; he or she chose the consequences. And the others behaved well.

You've got to be consistent in your use of consequences. You've got to be believable.

For consequences to work they need to be (1) immediate, so the child connects the unacceptable behavior with the result. They also need to be (2) given by a parent who is firm in sticking to the rule. It's best if (3) the consequences relate to the offense. It doesn't make sense for a child to lose his skateboard because of fighting with his brother, for instance.

A consequence is not punishment; it is the logical result of a child's choice. As one author put it, "You're just taking pleasure away, you're denying him the right to move until his other responsibilities are completed."[14]

Make your time limits reasonable. Consequences that are brief are better than ones that are long-term. If your child is disruptive, ten minutes by himself is a better learning experience than two hours. After more than ten minutes, the child will have found something interesting to think about or do, and the lesson will be lost.

Some consequences are natural. If your child has been told to keep his cookies on the table so the dog won't eat them, and he puts them on the floor, he will learn to follow instructions—unless you give him more cookies out of sympathy. All you have to say is, "When the dog eats the cookies, they're gone."

If your child has a pattern of oversleeping, missing his ride, and then having you take him to school, he's being indulged. He needs to experience the natural consequences. What are they? The authors of *Parenting with Love and Logic* have an excellent example:

> One day when David roared downstairs twenty minutes before school was to start, warmly yet firmly [Mom] said, "Oh, glad to see you're up. What do you think you'll do today in your room?"
>
> "In my room?" David said. "I'm going to school."
>
> "Well, that's good," Mom said. "How are you going to get there? The bus left ten minutes ago."
>
> "You're going to take me, of course," David replied.

> "Oh, sorry," Mom said. "I can't do that. I'll be busy with my housework all day. Feel free to arrange other transportation, or to spend the rest of the day in your room so I can do my work without any interruptions, just like other school days."
>
> "When lunch time comes, feel free to make something for yourself," Mom continued. "And if I go on any errands this afternoon, I'll take care of getting a babysitter for you. But don't worry if you can't pay the sitter. You can pay me back later in the week, or I can take it out on an errand. So it's not a problem right now.
>
> "Have a nice day, David. I'll see you at 3:30 when you normally get home on the bus."
>
> Of course, when the next morning rolls around and David wants an excuse note, Mom will say, "Oh, I can understand that. I know how nice a note is to explain why you were absent from school. But you know I only write notes for you when you're sick. Hope it works out okay with your teacher, though. Have a nice day, under the circumstances."[15]

There are also logical consequences that are arranged by you and are related to the situation. Whatever you say needs to be said not as a punishment, but as a choice. It needs to be applied immediately and in a calm voice.

"Sally, you can share your new game with your sister by each playing one round, or the game can be put away. Which would you like to do?"

"Jim, you can use your skateboard if you wear your knee pads and helmet. If you don't remember to wear them, there will be no riding. It's your choice."[16]

By the way, what are the rules for your children? Are they created as you go along, or have they been thoughtfully planned in advance? Parents are the decision makers for what is and isn't done or allowed. Many children would like to be, but they don't have the capability or resources to make the decisions. The parents need to keep the power.

Have you thought through rules about TV, movies, music, activities, outings, phone use, amount of time spent in homes of other children, supervision in those homes, involvement with friends, etc.? These will have to be faced at one time or another.

Some parents opt for many rules with little or inconsistent reinforcement. Some have a few rules with firm enforcement. It's important to pick your battles. Is what you're asking really all that important? How important is this on a scale of 0–10? Is this really going to matter a week from now?

Limits, consequences, and choices do work. One mother described her hassles with her young children. She said, "They always seem to act up at a restaurant or when we're buying groceries. When they were three and four we came up with a plan. We created these cardboard tickets and each time a child acted up we gave him one. Each ticket was worth five minutes sitting when we arrived home. If they ended up with three tickets and we had to leave a place early, they also earned an early bedtime. At first we gave out a lot of tickets. They soon learned that they had a choice whether to earn tickets or not."

Another mother was bothered about having to complain at the boys to get them to pick up after themselves. "Nothing seemed to work until we sat down and I told them about a new rule that was going into effect. It was a great opportunity for them to save money. For everything of theirs I had to pick up I charged them a dollar. There was no arguing. They knew the rule. It was their choice. Our place is much neater and I'm much happier."[17]

MAKING REQUESTS OF YOUR KIDS

A big part of teaching and training as a parent is giving requests. Have you ever listened to the way you make a request to your child?

When you give a request, don't use a rhetorical question. This type of question is not really a question. It's an implied request that is hidden or camouflaged. Some of these questions have shame or guilt attached to them.

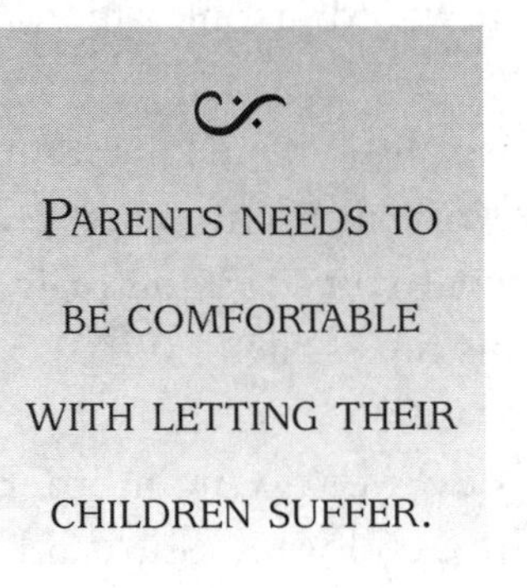

Have you ever gone into your child's room after requesting that she clean it, only to find it still a mess? If you're like most parents, you said, "Why is your room still messy?" But is that what you're really after? Do you really want to know why it wasn't cleaned or do you know the answer to that already? What is the issue you really want to address?

What about the question, "When are you going to grow up?" Are you looking for an answer? How would you respond if your child gave you an answer to that question? What if he took it at face value and said, "Well, in terms of growing up I think I'll wait a couple of years because I enjoy what I'm doing." Would you get upset at this response, accuse your child of being a smart mouth, and then punish him? If so, why? He answered your question.

What if you asked your child to do something, and she said she forgot? Some parents would want their children to stop what they're doing, go complete the forgotten task immediately, and that's what they would request. But others might say, "How could anyone forget that?" Questions like this invite defensive answers, smart-mouth answers, or "I don't know." Probably underneath this question is the thought, "How could anyone be that scatterbrained! My child is so irresponsible. I can't depend on her for anything." Your child most likely knows this.

Some parents hope by using questions in this way their children will take the hint and follow through. I wouldn't count on it. You've got to spell it out.

By the way, are you a solution giver? Some of us are more than others. We just love to fix the problems children encounter. After all, we're older, have more wisdom, experience, etc. We can do it more quickly. Unfortunately, this can keep our children tied to us and prevent them from solving problems on their own in the future.

Sometimes parents interfere with children experiencing consequences by jumping in before they can teach the lesson they were supposed to teach. If children wait until they are adults to learn these lessons, the results could be serious, and no one will be there to bail them out.

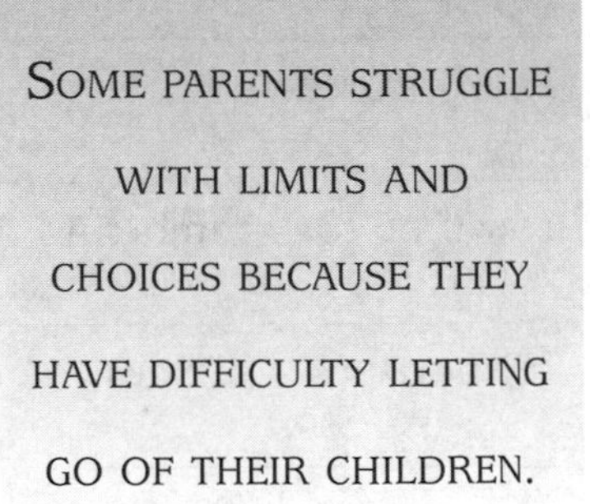

Consider this: How do you feel when your child suffers? Some parents can handle this, others rescue. Parents need to be comfortable with letting their children suffer. Consider this Scripture: "No discipline seems pleasant at the time, but painful. Later on, however, it produces a harvest of righteousness and peace for those who have been trained by it" (Heb. 12:11).

In order to learn consequences they need to be experienced.[18]

John Gray has suggested the five-second pause when your child brings a problem to you. Let your child feel what he is feeling for five seconds, then reflect back what you think he is feeling. This lets him know you understand and that it's okay for him to be feeling this way. It also lets him know that life will not always be the way he wants it to be.

Even if your child says, "I don't know what to do," he may not be ready for a solution. Wait him out. If your child says, "But you don't understand," don't argue with him. We probably *don't* understand what he or she is feeling. Have you ever said, "I think you're right, I probably don't understand, tell me again"?[19]

Here are some typical solutions as well as alternate responses:

GIVING A SOLUTION	**EMPATHIZING** Pause five seconds then say:
Don't cry.	I know it's disappointing.
Don't worry.	It is difficult. I know you are worried.
It will be okay tomorrow.	It is hard. I know you're disappointed.
It's not such a big deal.	I know you feel hurt. Let me give you a hug.
Hey, you can't win them all.	I know you're sad. I would be sad too.
It could be a lot worse.	I can see you're afraid. I would be afraid too.
You'll do fine.	Everything will be all right. I know you're scared. It's scary.
It's not that important anyway.	It's okay to be jealous. I would feel jealous too.
You'll get another chance.	If that happened to me, I would be disappointed too.[20]

Some parents struggle with limits and choices because they have difficulty letting go of their children. You might ask yourself these questions each morning:

What little tasks in my child's life am I holding on to that both of us are really ready for me to turn over to her?

For what activities might my child need or want a bit more instruction or further demonstration before I turn over the reins for that activity?

In areas my child is experiencing now, is there any follow-up I need to do, or any pointers I could share with him?

Is there any area of stress between us where I'm holding on too tightly?

Is there any area of stress where I'm assuming too early that it's time to let go?[21]

What limits do you need to set for your children? Yes, they'll resist—but a consistent, soft, yet definite approach on your part can give your child the structure and security he needs. And you can do it.

12

Secret 12

Great Parents Stay Focused on the Final Goal

A good name is rather to be chosen than great riches, and loving favor rather than silver and gold" (Prov. 22:1 AB).

Remember this verse? It's the conclusion to chapter 1. And it's the great parent's goal for his or her children—to be unique, to stand apart, to be a Christian nonconformist. Secure, unconditionally loved, nonindulged children have the best foundation to become people of integrity. We've been studying how to help our children become responsible—a responsible person has integrity. And that's the long-range goal we are working towards as parents.

Integrity is an active word. Proverbs 11:3 tells us, "The integrity of the upright guides them." The word describes an individual moving forward, confident in where he or she is going because of walking in the light of God's Word.[1]

The word as it's used in the Bible carries the meaning of being "sound, complete, without blemish, crack, or defeat." During biblical times, they didn't have Corningware or Noritake china. People relied on clay dishes, cups, and pots. It took many hours for a potter to shape, fire the dish (in a handmade kiln), and cool the piece. Unfortunately, with the uneven heat of a wood-fired furnace, cracks would often show up in the clay during the cooling process.

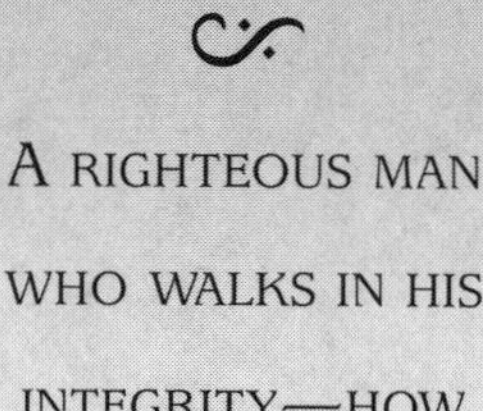

A RIGHTEOUS MAN WHO WALKS IN HIS INTEGRITY—HOW BLESSED ARE HIS SONS AFTER HIM. (PROV. 20:7 NASB)

A true craftsman would shatter the blemished piece and start over. An unscrupulous potter would fill in the cracks with wax and paint over the whole thing. The cracked vessel might hold up fine the first few times it was used. But if something really hot was placed inside it, the wax would soon melt and expose the defect.

That's why honest potters began putting the inscription "Without Wax" on the bottom of their pots. It was an inscription that meant this was a vessel that had been skillfully made, had been through the fires, and would stand the test of time. It was a vessel of integrity.

God's Word has much to say about this. Integrity can move us up the ladder the right way: "I put in charge of Jerusalem my brother Hanani, along with Hananiah the commander of the citadel, because he was a man of integrity and feared God more than most men do" (Neh. 7:2). Being a person of integrity can cost you points in the world's eyes. In God's view, it's the quickest and clearest way to follow his teaching.

Integrity brings us clear guidance: "The integrity of the upright guides them, but the unfaithful are destroyed by their duplicity" (Prov. 11:3).

Integrity provides a nonslip surface for our feet: "The days of the blameless are known to the LORD, and their inheritance will endure forever" (Ps. 37:18).

Integrity gives an unfailing blessing to our children: "A righteous man who walks in his integrity—how blessed are his sons after him" (Prov. 20:7 NASB).

Integrity makes a poor person rich: "Better is a poor man who walks in his integrity than he who is perverse in speech and is a fool" (Prov. 19:1 NASB).

Integrity makes all people better: "For the LORD God is a sun and shield; the LORD gives grace and glory; no good thing does He withhold from those who walk uprightly" (Ps. 84:11 NASB).

Integrity passes the test of what pleases God: "I know, my God, that you test the heart and are pleased with integrity" (1 Chron. 29:17).

Integrity makes us more like our Savior: "'Teacher,' they said, 'we know you are a man of integrity'" (Matt. 22:16).

If you want to know how integrity is lived out, consider this story of one mother:

"My son was in high school, and one day he told me, 'I won't be going to school this morning.'

'Why? Are you sick?'

'No, but it's national bank day, otherwise known as senior skip day, and everybody will be out of school.'

'Well, everybody else may be out, but you'd better be there.' And he left. We had an assistant principal who insisted that if your child was home it'd better be by your permission, and you had to notify him. If not, he'd call you. About nine thirty that evening the telephone rang, and it was the principal. He asked, 'Is John sick?'

'I don't understand. What do you mean, "Is John sick?"'

'Well, he wasn't in school today, and you didn't call.'

Then it hit me, and I said, 'Well, he disobeyed me, because I told him to be in school.'

The principal said, 'You know I'm going to have to discipline him.'

'You take care of him on that end, and I'll take care of him on this end,' I said.

So I confronted John: 'Why weren't you in school today?'

'Well, nobody else was there.'

I was angry. 'I don't care about everybody else. You were to be in school.' So I punished him by grounding him for quite a while.

> IF ANY OF YOU LACKS WISDOM, HE SHOULD ASK GOD, WHO GIVES GENEROUSLY TO ALL.
>
> (JAMES 1:5)

The next day he walked out the door angry and mumbling. When he came back that afternoon, I figured he'd still be sulking. He wasn't, but he just kept walking slowly around the house. Finally he said, 'Thank you.'

I looked to see who he was talking to and said, 'Pardon me?'

'Thank you.'

'For what?'

'I stood ten feet tall today. The principal told me that he began calling parents at eight in the morning and finished at ten that night, talking to every parent whose child had skipped school. And he said, "Your mother is the only one who told the truth."' Then John said, 'And I thank you for that.'"[2]

THIS IS INTEGRITY

As they go through life, your children are going to be faced with a multitude of decisions. And they're not the decisions of a few generations ago! Will they say yes or no to drugs? Will they say yes or no to premarital sex? Will they say yes or no to an attractive cult leader? Will they say yes or no to the wrong person to marry? There will be times when they, like you, will need insight, wisdom, and help.

It's frightening to think about all the present and future decisions your children will have to make. What if they end up just drifting through school or into some "job" with little or no meaning? What if they never tap into and activate the potential that God has given them?

But don't let yourself panic. Now isn't the time to ask, "What if ..." and end up worrying. Right decisions come from wisdom and discernment. James 1:5 tells us these qualities come from God: "If any of you lacks wisdom, he should ask God, who gives generously to all without finding fault, and it will be given to him."

WISDOM WILL SAVE YOU FROM THE WAYS OF WICKED MEN. (PROV. 2:12)

Read, study, and memorize God's Word. Pray for wisdom for you and your children. And consider these words:

> Trust in the LORD with all your heart and lean not on your own understanding; in all your ways acknowledge him, and he will make your paths straight. (Prov. 3:5–6)

> Wisdom is supreme; therefore get wisdom. Though it cost all you have, get understanding. Esteem her, and she will exalt you; embrace her, and she will honor you. (Prov. 4:7–8)

> For wisdom will enter your heart, and knowledge will be pleasant to your soul. Discretion will protect

> you, and understanding will guard you. Wisdom will save you from the ways of wicked men, from men whose words are perverse. (Prov. 2:10–12)

The best way for your children to learn to value and pursue wisdom is for them to see you doing so. Be a model of integrity as John's mother was.

You see, once again we go back to modeling. If we want a character trait developed within our children, the best opportunity for this to occur is experiencing it in our home.

I came across a summation of studies that shows what much of this book has been about. It demonstrated that responsible children tended to come from homes that included the following:

> There was an atmosphere of warmth in the family expressed by love, affection, affirmations, interest in the child's life, positive feedback, and appropriate praise. Can you give an example of this in your family?
>
> These homes also demonstrated firm control. There were clear rules about important issues. Not only that the children understood the rules, they could state them and knew what the consequences were. Discussion and reasoning were used first, and if these weren't effective, they progressed to isolation, denial of privileges, and then restriction of freedom. What would your child say the rules are in your home?
>
> Third, there was no enmeshment (or too much emotional involvement). Parents did not see their children as extensions of themselves. There was a healthy level of emotional attachment. The children had their world and the parents their own world. There were proper boundaries. These parents knew how not to be influenced by their child's anger, verbal attacks, or plays to make them feel guilty about discipline.

> Consistency was a major factor in terms of rules. Both parents were consistent with one another as well as with their children. There was no difference between what the parent asked the child to do and what the parents did.
>
> Decision making and choice evaluation were taught. The children were invited to speak their minds, give opinions, evaluate options and choices—in other words, there was a strong emphasis upon learning to think for oneself and make choices. Phrases like "What do you think?" or "Had you considered …?" or "What are some other possibilities?" or "If a friend offered this, what could you say?" were frequent expressions.
>
> Independence was promoted in all areas according to age level. There was a belief in "you can do it" messages and this was conveyed to the child. There was also a holding back from rescuing the child when the going was tough. Age-appropriate responsibilities were given with expectations that each child would be a contributing family member. Immature or childish behavior was discouraged.
>
> Parents encouraged their children to become socialized—to learn to get along with others as well as follow the rules of society. Impulse control was taught and no physical or verbal abuse was tolerated. Respect, politeness, and good manners were a part of family life.
>
> A final characteristic that was surprising was nonconformity. It was actually encouraged. Peer pressure did not influence. Children from these homes tended to be willing to be different since they had their own principles.[3]

Jesus preached and practiced nonconformity. He was different. If you teach this you'll be saying, "Don't conform. Don't go along with everything." That's really what being a Christian is all about. Too often we don't stick out enough. But today a person of integrity really will!

If someone asked you, "What do you want your children to be known for?" what would you say? What kind of reputation do you want them to have? A label or series of descriptive adjectives, once applied, seems to stick to us like Super Glue. Most parents want their children to be known for doing what is right. But the question is, by whose standards? There are many sets of values in operation in our world today.

The Bible is the standard that great parents want their children to follow. That standard can be summed up in one word: purity. It's a manifestation of integrity—no wax! Not only does Proverbs talk about that, but so did Paul. He said, "Keep yourself pure" (1 Tim. 5:22 NKJV). That's hard because it means you have to go counterculture. And if you think it's difficult for an adult to do that, imagine what it must be like for a child. You see, being pure means being free from anything that taints, impairs, or infects—free from defects and sin. That's asking a lot!

Can kids have a pure life in the world that we live in? Yes, they can. But they must be in submission to God and his Holy Spirit. What can you do as a parent to help your children? We've talked about many steps throughout this book. But underlying every new and different approach has to be one other element—prayer. The author of *The Power of a Praying Parent* suggests this:

> Let's pray for our children to be attracted to holiness and purity like a magnet, so that when anything entices them that isn't holy or pure, they detect the pull immediately and are made uncomfortable enough to thoroughly reject it. "For God did not call us to uncleanness, but in holiness" (1 Thessalonians 4:7 [NKJV]). To live purely within the boundaries of God's law is to find wholeness in

> the total person. That wholeness is what holiness is all about. Children who have a desire for holiness and seek God's enabling power to help them achieve it can never be anything but blessed and fulfilled.[4]

There's one other way for our children to really stand out and be nonconformists in today's society—by having a loving relationship with Jesus. It's not just acknowledging him, knowing him, believing in him, or serving him. It's loving him. Often parents ask, "What can we do to raise children who are not only competent and responsible people of integrity, but also who love Jesus? Well, does your child see others loving Jesus and talking openly about loving Jesus? Ken Gire tells about someone who taught him to love Jesus:

> The difference a person can make in your life, if that person really loves you, is extraordinary. I think of my grandmother, who loved me like that. She was always fun to be around because she laughed a lot and teased a lot and you never got in her way, a fairly frequent thing kids get into when around adults. But not around this adult. Not with her grandkids, anyway. She rolled bandages for missionaries from strips of bedsheets, which is one of the things I remember when we visited her. When she visited us, which was once a year, she brought a bulging suitcase, complete with all her medications, which included Peppermint Schnapps, and of course "a little something" for each of us, candy or a coloring book or a little something she picked up somewhere and saved for one of her visits. She filled the house with the aroma of things she baked from scratch, and Canasta, which she taught us kids and brought us into the game around the table with the adults. She also filled the house with stories about Jesus. Invariably, one of those stories was

> about someone she met on the airplane on her way to visit us. Whenever she traveled, she always struck up conversations with whoever was seated next to her. And it didn't make any difference who it was, high school drop-out or corporate executive, her conversations always led to one question: "Do you love the Lord?" she would ask them. Not know him, not believe in him, but "Do you love him?"
>
> She, of course, asked me the very same question every time she visited. And of course I said yes, little knowing what all was involved in loving someone I couldn't hug or play Canasta with. I always said yes, I think as I reflect on it now, because I didn't want to disappoint her. I knew that loving the Lord was important to her, and since I loved her, that made it important to me. Not overnight, but over the years. Love has a way of rubbing off like that.
>
> Who knows what spiritual energy lay dormant in that question she had planted in my young heart. Maybe something of that energy was what landed me in seminary. As I look back on my memories of her, she seemed to have the right emphasis, not only in the way she worded the question but in the way she lived her life. Though she is gone now, the way she lived her life lives with me still.
>
> So does her question.[5]

May "Do you love Jesus?" be the guiding question you use in training your child to be a responsible, loving servant of Jesus Christ. Then you truly will be a great parent for your kids.

Readers' Guide

For Personal Reflection and Group Discussion

Entitlement

Big word. Big problem. You live in a world where children are taught to expect a certain standard of living. Younger children believe they ought to have all the toys so generously presented in those commercials stuffed in between kids' shows that are often nothing more than extended commercials themselves. Older children count on you to step in and fix their problems—like doing an extra load of laundry at midnight because they just have to wear that blue and white sweatshirt the next day. It's the age of entitlement, and you're the one called upon to respond to that cry.

When you respond to that cry with unregulated giving or by making your children the very center of your life, home, and schedule, you may discover one day that your children have suddenly become … wait for it … spoiled!

This book is an antidote to a spoiled or indulged child. If you're like most parents, you already know what it's like to lose control of your children. How do you regain control? And how can you turn a frustrated, ungrateful child into one who is responsible and striving for integrity?

Well, you've started things right by picking up this book. It's packed with practical advice and anecdotes to help you deal with the age of entitlement in your own home.

The questions that follow are designed to help you examine your specific parenting situation and uncover spiritual and practical truths that can help prepare your children to grow into responsible adults who love God and desire to follow Jesus. Use these questions for personal reflection, as a discussion-starter for you and your spouse, or in a small group setting. Then take what you learn and apply it. Not only will you feel better about parenting, your children will thank you too. (Maybe not right away, but someday.)

SECRET 1
GREAT PARENTS KNOW THEY CAN'T DO IT ALONE

1. How does it make you feel to know that you can't be a great parent without God's help? Describe your emotions, and explain why you feel the way you do.

2. If your children truly are "on loan" to you from God, how does that affect your attitude and your actions in parenting them?

3. "As parents, we need to pray constantly for our children. You want to saturate your child in prayer." What obstacles keep you from "saturating" your children in prayer? What could you do this week to help overcome those obstacles?

4. When was the last time you prayed Scripture over your children? What happened? When will be the next time you pray Scripture over your children? What do you expect will come of those prayers?

5. What do you see as the benefits of keeping a prayer journal for your kids? Are you willing to try a prayer journal for the next seven days? If yes, begin today!

SECRET 2
GREAT PARENTS UNDERSTAND THE UNIQUE PRESSURES OF GROWING UP IN AMERICA

1. One of the foundational concepts in this book is captured in this sentence: "Parenting involves embarking upon a lifetime of transformation." What is your initial reaction to this statement? How has this been true for you?

2. Consider *The 8 Seasons of Parenthood*, which are described beginning on page 26 of this chapter. Which season are you in now? Are you in multiple seasons at once? How accurately do these seasons describe your life situation?

3. Respond to the following comment: "During the second half of the last century, something happened to the family. It seems as though control shifted from the parents to the children." In what ways have you seen this to be true? How has that affected your ability to parent?

4. Wright states that we can't produce a perfect life for our children, but "we can work at preparing them to live their lives in an imperfect world." What role does your personal relationship with Jesus play in that preparation? How do you model and teach your children about the eternal importance of a relationship with Jesus?

5. Think about your own childhood. Were you a "child of entitlement"? How about your children? What does this tell you about the world in which today's children live? What challenges does this pose for you as a parent?

6. Read Luke 16:13. How have you struggled with living out this truth in your own life? If your children learn habits and behaviors from you, what are they learning today? What do you want them to learn?

7. Proverbs 22:1 states that a good name is better than riches. How do you support this in your parenting? What does "a good name" mean in today's society?

SECRET 3
GREAT PARENTS UNDERSTAND THE CONSEQUENCES OF OVERINDULGENCE

1. What is the first image that comes to mind when you read or hear the word *spoiled*? Do you agree that a coddled or spoiled child is destined to be an underdeveloped person? Explain your answer.

2. Think about that familiar statement "I'm bored." How many times have you heard that from your children? How does this reflect an inability of the children to entertain themselves? In what ways have you contributed to this lack of initiative?

3. What are some specific examples from your household that illustrate what an "indulged child" looks like? Why is it important for children to learn to stick to tasks and become problem solvers and take appropriate risks? Do you find it easy to stick to tasks, problem solve, or take appropriate risks? Look back on your own childhood to see why you might act this way.

4. One of Wright's propositions is that for an adult to make it through life, he or she needs to be "resistant and resourceful." What does that look like in your own life? How are you instilling that truth in your children? Imagine your child as an adult, but with the behaviors he or she expresses today. How would your child respond to the stresses of the workplace? The challenges of maintaining a household? Of nurturing relationships? Then consider your reaction to these thoughts. Are you more hopeful or afraid? What ideas do you have to swing the pendulum more to hope?

5. Reflect on the prayer life of your children. What is the main focus of their prayers? Is it for God to give them things or solve problems for them? Compare their prayers to your own. How much of your prayer time is spent in worship or thankfulness or confession? A prayer life focused on "give me, give me" probably indicates an indulged child (or adult).

6. Look at the list of principles on page 60. Which of these stands out to you as something you do well as a parent? Which are you struggling with? Reflect on Galatians 6:9, then take some time to pray for perseverance in parenting. If you are discussing this in a small group, talk with group members about how you can support one another's efforts to live out these principles.

SECRET 4
GREAT PARENTS GIVE ... BUT NOT TOO MUCH

1. What was your initial reaction to the opening anecdote about John and his mother? Can you see ways in which your value is tied to your children needing you? Describe these. Wright suggests centering your world around a child can be a negative thing. What is a better way to describe a parent's responsibility in caring for his or her children?

2. Read the Driving Agreement on pages 65–66. How would your children react to something like this? If they're not driving age, consider a similar kind of document for household chores. If you imagine significant resistance to this sort of thing, what does that tell you about your children? What steps would it take to move your children toward a pattern of life that would accept (and perhaps even embrace) this sort of responsible thinking?

3. Make a list of all the household help each of your children provides. How well do they follow through with these chores? What does the length of your list or your answer to the second question say about how coddled your children are? If you're not happy with your conclusion, what ideas do you have to change this?

4. Think about a time when you rescued your child from some consequence. Maybe you helped with a last-minute school project or placed a phone call he or she should have made. What was the child's request or need? How would he have handled the situation without your rescue? What made it difficult for you to let him fail or deal with the situation alone? Though this is an extreme example, think about Jesus' request of God in the garden of Gethsemane when he asked God to "take this cup from me." What would the world look like if God had indeed rescued Jesus from the cross?

5. What role (if any) does guilt play in your parenting? What are the dangers of allowing guilt to drive your parenting style? How can your guilt negatively affect your children's ability to grow and learn responsibility? Have you ever substituted "things" for time? What prompted that decision? How can you avoid repeating that behavior in the future?

6. What is your reaction to Wright's comments about the two-income family? Do you agree or disagree? If you disagree, what reasons would you give for why it's important to have both parents working?

7. Are your children hurrying through life? What are some examples to support your answer? How does your "hurriedness" compare to your children's? Read the story of Mary and Martha in Luke 10:38–42. In what way is this a story about hurriedness?

SECRET 5
GREAT PARENTS CHALLENGE THEIR KIDS ... BUT NOT TOO MUCH

1. Do you know (or are you) parents who don't let their children be children? What does that look like? How does catering to your children's world keep them from learning real-life lessons? When was the last time your children cried out, "That's not fair!"? How did you respond?

2. If your children are in sports or other similar activities, are they having fun? How much of their experience is more important to you than to them? What is the fine line between encouraging children and pressuring them? How have you crossed that line, and how can you adjust if necessary to step back into encouragement?

3. Why is it often difficult for parents to accept it when their children turn out to be "average" in academics? How does your own academic experience influence the way you talk to your children about school? The expectations you have for them? What are some ways you can celebrate your "average" children so they don't feel average at all, but unique and valuable to you and to God?

4. What is your reaction to Wright's comments about R-rated movies? Do you agree or disagree? How does Romans 12 apply to the world of entertainment and your children? React to this statement: "If we aren't comfortable watching something with our children, maybe we shouldn't be watching it."

5. Which of the three roles of parenting (Protector, Chum, Realist) are you experiencing right now? If you've experienced more than one, which is the most challenging for you? How do you juggle different roles simultaneously? Why is it important to relinquish control as children are able to take on more responsibility?

6. If your role as parent is to "cooperate with, not to supercede, God's plan and design" for your children, what changes might you have to make to your current parenting style? Consider any areas where you might be pushing your children. Then talk with your spouse or a close friend (or group member) and come up with some practical ways you can parent instead of push.

SECRET 6
GREAT PARENTS KNOW HOW TO AVOID SPOILING THEIR CHILDREN

1. Take a look at the list of ways you can create an indulged child on pages 104–105 of this chapter. Can you think of a time you did these with your own children? Which is the most difficult action for you to avoid? Why do you think that is true for you?

2. Which role is more difficult for you, Teacher-Coach or Leader-Guide? How do you know when to act out these different roles? What happens when you try to be a Teacher-Coach when a Leader-Guide is called for? Think back on the best examples of someone who has taught or led you. What made those experiences particularly memorable? What can you learn from this to apply to your parenting?

3. Some parents play the role of Friend-Companion at the expense of other roles. What are the potential negative impacts of doing this? How can you determine when the role of Friend-Companion is appropriate and when it isn't?

4. Is it easy or difficult for you to say no to your children? If it is difficult for you, what makes it so? Look at the phrases on pages 113–114 and then think about some situations where you might use them. Come up with a few of your own as well.

5. If you were to describe your child's life, which word would you use: simple or cluttered? When Jesus called the

disciples, he asked them to drop what they were doing and follow him. Some left careers that would have earned them a decent living, and all traded their former lives for a simpler existence. What are some ways you and your children could simplify your lives? What benefits do you see from doing this?

6. As you consider the command in Ephesians 6:4, to bring up your children "in the training and instruction of the Lord," how would you rate your success so far? What are some things you think you could improve? What are some things you're doing well? Ask God for continued guidance and wisdom in how to raise your children so they aren't spoiled.

Secret 7
Great Parents Work to Be Great Communicators

1. Think about some of the things you've said to your children that fall into the category of "silly questions" like "Are you going to stop it?" or "Do you want me to send you to a time-out?" What prompts this kind of question? What value, if any, is there in a question like this? Come up with some alternative ways to say what you really mean.

2. Make a list of clichés you use in parenting your children. What is the real message you're trying to get across with these clichés? Make a new list of a few ways you can say what you mean without using a cliché. How can this keep your children from tuning you out because they've "heard it a thousand times"?

3. Do you know your children's learning styles? If you have more than one child, do they each have a different style? What does that suggest about how you should communicate with your children? Think of a message you typically might want to give to your children, then come up with ways to express that instruction to visual, auditory, and kinesthetic learners.

4. Read the scripture passages on pages 129–130. Which passage has the most immediate impact on you? Do you think the author of Proverbs is too harsh with the statement that "there is more hope for a fool" than for someone who is hasty in his words? Why or why not? Think of a time you have been on the receiving end of negative words. What did that feel like? What can you learn from that experience that can help you avoid the same choices in your parenting role?

5. What does your self-talk sound like? What is your inner conversation when you're communicating with your children? How does the truth of Proverbs 23:7 play out in your life? Read Philippians 4:8 and prayerfully consider what this verse has to say about your self-talk.

Secret 8
Great Parents Know How to Use the Tools of Listening and Timing

1. Psalm 116:1–2 tells us that God listens to us. How does that impact the way you relate to God? What does this tell you about the importance of listening? Describe the positive benefits of being truly listened to, then consider how those benefits could impact your children.

2. Re-read the three-part definition of what listening really means on pages 138–139 of this chapter. How well are you doing these things in your relationships with other adults? How about with your children? Is there a difference between the two? If so, what is different and why?

3. The author describes five basic reasons why "we ought to listen" to our children. Read them on page 140 of this chapter and think of a recent example when you listened to your child. How many of these reasons apply to that one example? Do you find yourself jumping to conclusions or finishing your child's thoughts sometimes? How does this thwart the reasons for listening?

4. Wright says that "listening is an expression of love." Consider how this is true for you—how you've experienced that love because someone listened to you. What are some ways you can express that same kind of love in communication with your children? What is the greatest challenge you face when trying to truly listen to your children?

5. It's important to choose the right time to communicate with your children. What are some examples of the "right time"? of the "wrong time"? What ideas do you have for creating a tradition—a "right time" that is both fun and safe for your children to communicate what's on their minds? Consider implementing these ideas.

6. Make a mental list of the positive messages you've given your children this past week. Compare that list to the one delineating all the negative things you said. What does this tell you about your communication with your children? How can you turn some of those negative messages around or rephrase them into positive messages?

SECRET 9
GREAT PARENTS PAY ATTENTION TO A CHILD'S EMOTIONS

1. The author writes that children need unconditional love more than any other emotion. What are some ways you've experienced unconditional love? How do you show this (and say it) to your children? What are the challenges to showing a child unconditional love?

2. Was your childhood one full of emotional expression or repressed emotions? How do you think that impacts the way you relate to your children? Wright states that treating children's feelings as trivial or unimportant can teach them that expressing feelings is wrong or a sign of weakness. Even if you're not naturally comfortable with expressing emotions, what can you do to acknowledge and encourage your children's emotional expression?

3. Go back and read the list of phrases you can use to reflect back to your child what you think he or she is feeling (on page 164). Have you used these phrases with your children? Which ones feel most natural to you? What is the benefit of using phrases like these in your communication? What skill does this model that could help your children when they're adults?

4. React to this statement: "Emotions are the real fuel source behind power struggles." How has this been true in your relationship with your children? How often is anger the source of a power struggle? Take some time to review the seven steps for helping your children deal with anger. What are some practical ways you can teach your children this approach?

5. Review a recent conversation with a child that included a strong emotional component. If you found yourself asking the "why" question, what was the child's response? What is so difficult about answering "why" in regard to emotional issues? Replay that situation and think of some "what" and "who" and "how" questions you could have asked. How do these kinds of questions show a real interest in your child's feelings?

Secret 10
Great Parents Avoid These Ten Steps to Disaster

1. This chapter focuses on disastrous approaches to parenting your children. Before you read this section, did you have a mental image of what some of these approaches might be? How many of these have you practiced in your parenting? Which do you struggle with most?

2. If you've ever uttered the words "how many times have I told you …?" you've probably fallen into the "repeating yourself" trap. Recall a time when you had to repeat your request to a child. Were you in the same room with the child? Were you making eye contact? What was the tone of your voice? What are some ways you could have handled the situation differently?

3. Have you attempted the "Broken Record Technique" for avoiding bargaining or quarrels? Was this easy or difficult for you? How did that go over with your child?

4. Many parents fall into the default mode of lecturing when relating to their children. If you do this, you probably also recognize the Parent Lecture Gaze. What are the characteristics of a lecture? How can simplifying your message change a lecture into something your child can learn from? What are some other ways to avoid this disaster?

5. Wright states that using any kind of fear response with your children actually brings about the opposite of what you want to happen. How has this been true for you? In what ways does using fear damage your relationship with your children? If you tend to use the fear approach, what can you do to change that?

SECRET 11
GREAT PARENTS LEARN TO BE LIMIT-SETTERS

1. When you read "It's all right to take care of yourself" on pages 190–191 of this chapter, what was your reaction? Relief? Disbelief? Review the past month and make a mental list of all the things you did to take care of yourself. How long is that list? How many of these things did your children notice? Why might it be important for your children to see that you have a life?

2. Read Proverbs 4:1–5 again. When you think of the word *wisdom*, what comes to mind? If experience brings wisdom, how can you benefit from wisdom if you're going through the parenting role for the first time? How can the wisdom of others help you make good parenting decisions? Think of someone you could talk to who might have some parenting wisdom to share. Keep in mind that while some wisdom is timeless, other wisdom may be so closely tied to the culture of the time that older parents might not be able to speak to every issue.

3. List two or three "child-type behaviors" your children have tried that could be added to Wes Haystead's list found on pages 193–194. When your children perform these sorts of not-too-bright escapades, how do you respond? If you played the role of "manager" in your parenting during these situations, how would that differ from the way you currently respond?

4. Write out how you feel about setting limits with your children. Do you find yourself more authoritarian or passive? How does the way you deal with limits compare to the way your parents treated you? What lessons can you learn from your parents or other parents you know about setting limits? Share with a friend (or small group member) about times when setting limits worked for you … and when it didn't.

5. How do you respond to the following statement: "One of the best ways for a child to learn to be insecure is for him to realize he has more power than his parents." What are some examples of this in your own parenting? How do children get more power than their parents? Perhaps you set limits, then move them according to what the child says or asks. Is that any different than not setting limits at all? Why or why not?

6. Review the Scriptures on pages 200–201, then practice offering empathy and correction with your spouse, a friend, or a small group member. How easy or difficult is it for you to offer empathy when your children do something that upsets you? If you think back to a time when you allowed a situation to escalate, what role (if any) did empathy play in that scenario? If you didn't express empathy, how could you have done so? What impact might that have had on the situation?

7. As an adult, you probably understand consequences all too well. What are some examples of circumstances in your own life where you learned from the consequences of a decision? Now recall the most recent situation in which your child could have (or did) learned from consequences. Was it easy to recall a time your child experienced consequences? Were those natural consequences or logical consequences? Take a little time to discuss with your spouse or a small group member about the rules you have in your house—and the natural and logical consequences that could apply to those rules.

Secret 12
Great Parents Stay Focused on the Final Goal

1. Without looking at what Dr. Wright has to say, come up with your own definition of "integrity." How can integrity "guide" you (as it states in Prov. 11:3)? What differences might there be in a worldly definition of integrity and one based on God's Word? Which definition do you strive to live by? What are some ways you can model this for your children?

2. Read Proverbs 3:5–6 again and reflect on these words. What does it mean to "lean not on your own understanding"? How would you interpret the promise that God will "make your paths straight" in light of the fact that life doesn't always go the way you plan or hope for?

3. Do you believe that nonconformity should be encouraged? Why or why not? What is the difference between affirming nonconformity and pressing children to be unique? It's not always easy to accept children's uniquenesses, particularly when they don't look anything like what you expected. What are some things your child does that could be considered nonconformity issues worth affirming? What are some that might call for correction?

4. Wright suggests that children can have a pure life in this world if they're in submission to God and his Holy Spirit. Do you agree or disagree? Explain your position. What are the greatest challenges your children face that push against the ability to live a pure life? It's important to challenge children to pursue a pure life, but it's also important to let kids know that's not the same as living a perfect life. Take some time this week to talk with your children about what it means to live in submission to God and his Holy Spirit.

5. Have you asked your children "Do you love Jesus?" How can you share with younger children what it means to love Jesus? What is the greatest way you can illustrate that love for older children and teenagers? Take a few minutes to pray for your children to learn to love Jesus. Then commit to showing them what that means by modeling your own love for Christ and teaching them about God's love for them.

NOTES

SECRET 1
GREAT PARENTS KNOW THEY CAN'T DO IT ALONE

1. John White, *Parents in Pain* (Downers Grove, IL: InterVarsity, 1979), 165.
2. Ibid., 164.
3. Stormie Omartian, *The Power of a Praying Parent* (Eugene, OR: Harvest House, 1995), 18–19.
4. John Bunyan, as quoted in GIGA Quotes. http://giga-usa.com/quotes/authors/john_bunyan_a001.htm.
5. Kent and Barbara Hughes, *Common Sense Parenting* (Wheaton, IL: Tyndale House, 1995), 91.
6. Oswald Chambers, *Daily Thoughts for Disciples* (Grand Rapids: Zondervan, 1975), 75.
7. Quin Sherrer and Ruthanne Garlock, *How to Pray for Your Children* (Ventura, CA: Regal Books, 1998), 33–34.
8. David and Heather Kopp, *Praying the Bible for Your Children* (Colorado Springs: Waterbrook Press, 1998), adapted, 10.
9. Ibid., 15–18.
10. Quin Sherrer and Ruthanne Garlock, *The Spiritual Warrior's Prayer Guide* (Ann Arbor, MI: Servant Publications, 1992), 156.
11. Hughes, *Common Sense Parenting,* 85.
12. Omartian, *The Power of a Praying Parent,* 13–14.
13. Quin Sherrer, *How to Pray for Your Children* (Edmonds, VA: Aglow Publications, 1986), 76.

14. Kopp, *Praying the Bible,* 161, 166.
15. Ronda De Sola Chervin, *A Mother's Treasury of Prayers* (Ann Arbor, MI: Servant Publications, 1994), 181. Adapted from Quin Sherrer and Ruthanne Garlock, *The Spiritual Warrior's Prayer Guide.*
16. Sherrer and Garlock, *How to Pray for Your Children*, selections from chapter 2.

Secret 2
Great Parents Understand the Unique Pressures of Growing Up in America

1. Barbara C. Unell and Jerry L. Wyckoff, *The 8 Seasons of Parenthood* (New York: Times Books, Random House, 2000), 95.
2. Ibid., 15–16, 61, 155, 193, 268, adapted.
3. Daniel Okrent, "Twilight of the Boomers," *Time*, June 12, 2000, 68–70, adapted.
4. Laura Schlessinger, *Parenthood by Proxy* (New York: Harper Collins, 2000), 197.
5. Daniel Okrent, "Twilight of the Boomers," *Time*, June 12, 2000, 68–70, adapted.
6. Ibid.
7. Leonard Pitts Jr., *Detroit Free Press*, June 10, 1999.
8. Elizabeth Ellis, *Raising a Responsible Child* (Secaucus, NJ: Citadel Press, 1996), 10, adapted.
9. *Los Angeles Times*, May 21, 1999, adapted.
10. Steve Farrar, *If I'm Not Tarzan and My Wife Isn't Jane, Then What Are We Doing in the Jungle?* (Portland, OR: Multnomah, 1991), 65–66, adapted.
11. "Bratlash! The Race to Raise Unspoiled Kids. Teaching Kids Middle Class Values," *Wall Street Journal Weekend Journal*, January 14, 2000, adapted.
12. "Making Heirs Work for Their Wealth," June 25, *Los Angeles Times*, Business section, adapted.

Secret 3
Great Parents Understand the Consequences of Overindulgence

1. Gary J. Oliver, *Made Perfect in Weakness* (Colorado Springs: Chariot Victor Publishing, 1995), 25, adapted.
2. Archibald Hart, *Stress and Your Child* (Dallas: Word Publishers, 1992), 228–29.
3. Elizabeth M. Ellis, *Raising a Responsible Child* (Secaucus, NY: Citadel Press, 1996), 41–58, adapted.
4. John Gray, *Children Are from Heaven* (New York: HarperCollins, 1998), 4–5.
5. Adapted from the following articles: David A. Kaplan, "The Best Happy Ending," *Newsweek*, February 28, 1994, 44–45; Paul A. Witteman, "Finally," *Time*, February 28, 1994; Alexander Wolff, "Whooosh!" *Sports Illustrated*, February 28, 1994, 19–23.

SECRET 4
GREAT PARENTS GIVE ... BUT NOT TOO MUCH

1. Diane Ehrensaft, *Spoiling Children* (New York: Guilford Press, 1997), 139–43, adapted.
2. Foster Cline and Jim Fay, *Parenting Teens with Love and Logic* (Colorado Springs: Nav Press, 1992), 30–31, adapted.
3. Ralph E. Minear and William Proctor, *Kids Who Have Too Much* (Nashville: Thomas Nelson, 1989), 105–110, adapted.
4. Ehrensaft, *Spoiling Children*, 81–91, adapted.
5. Nancy Samalin, *Loving Your Child Is Not Enough* (New York: Penguin Books, 1998), xii–xiii, adapted.
6. "Lies Parents Tell Themselves About Why They Work," *U.S. News and World Report*, May 12, 1997, 59–60, adapted.
7. Bob Welch, *More to Life Than Having It All* (Eugene, OR: Harvest House, 1991), 36–37.
8. Ehrensaft, 130–34, adapted.
9. Ehrensaft, 137.

SECRET 5
GREAT PARENTS CHALLENGE THEIR KIDS ... BUT NOT TOO MUCH

1. Alvin Rosenfeld and Nicole Wise, *Hyper-Parenting* (New York: St. Martin's Press, 2000), 139, adapted.
2. Ibid., 188–89, adapted.
3. Sandy Banks, "Even Sports Are No Longer About Play," *Los Angeles Times*, June 16, 2000, Southern California Living Section E, 1–2, adapted.
4. Dana Scott Spears and Ron L. Braund, *Strong-Willed Child or Dreamer* (Nashville: Thomas Nelson, 1996).
5. Rosenfeld and Wise, *Hyper-Parenting*, 203.
6. Sandy Banks, "What Are Boomer Parents Teaching Kids?" *L.A. Times*, August 15, 2000, 1–3, adapted.
7. H. Norman Wright, *Communication: Key to Your Marriage* (Ventura, CA: Regal Books, 2000).
8. Rosenfeld and Wise, *Hyper-Parenting*, 183, adapted.
9. Ron Taffel, *Parenting by Heart* (New York: Addison-Wesley Publishing, 1991), 6–11, adapted.
10. Ibid., 46–48, adapted.
11. Becky A. Bailey, *Easy to Love, Difficult to Discipline* (New York: William Morrow & Co., 2000), 190–96, adapted.
12. Rosenfeld and Wise, *Hyper-Parenting*, 116–17, adapted.
13. Ibid., 53–54, 109–110, adapted.
14. Ralph Mattson and Thom Black, *Discovering Your Child's Design* (Colorado Springs: David C. Cook Publishing Co., 1989), 189–91, adapted.

SECRET 6
GREAT PARENTS KNOW HOW TO AVOID SPOILING THEIR CHILDREN

1. Fred Gosman, *Spoiled Rotten* (New York: Warner Books, 1990), 51, adapted.

2. Ibid., 106–7, adapted.
3. Ron Taffel, *Parenting by Heart* (New York: Addison-Wesley Publishing, 1991), 199–203, adapted.
4. David Domico, *The Influential Parent* (Wheaton, IL: Shaw Publishers, 1997), 96–114, adapted.
5. Gosman, *Spoiled Rotten,* 118–20, adapted.
6. Paul and Jeannie McKean, *Leading a Child to Independence* (San Bernardino, CA: Here's Life Publishers, 1986), 21.
7. Ibid., 21–23, adapted.
8. Ibid., 134–35.
9. Ibid., 144–45.
10. Tony and Bart Campolo, *Things We Wish We Had Said* (Dallas: Word Publishing, 1989), 63.

SECRET 7
GREAT PARENTS WORK TO BE GREAT COMMUNICATORS

1. Denis Donovan and Deborah McIntyre, *What Did I Just Say?* (New York: Henry Holt, 1999), 7–8, adapted.
2. Donovan and McIntyre, *What Did,* 144–52, adapted.
3. John Gray, *Children Are From Heaven* (New York: HarperCollins, 1998), 40–42, adapted.
4. Ibid.
5. Mary Sheedy Kurcinka, *Kids, Parents, and Power Struggles* (New York: HarperCollins, 2000).

SECRET 8
GREAT PARENTS KNOW HOW TO USE THE TOOLS OF LISTENING AND TIMING

1. Denis Donovan and Deborah McIntyre, *What Did I Just Say?* (New York: Henry Holt & Co., 1999), 141–46, adapted.
2. Ray Guarendi, *Back to the Family* (New York: Villard Books, 1990), 142–43, adapted.
3. Leonard Zunin and Natalie Zunin, *Contact: The First Four Minutes* (New York: Ballantine Books, 1972), 150–52, adapted.
4. Ibid., 154–55, adapted.
5. Donovan and McIntyre, *What Did,* 141–146, adapted.
6. Josh McDowell and Dick Day, *How to Be a Hero to Your Kids* (Waco, TX: Word Publishing, 1991), 87–88.

SECRET 9
GREAT PARENTS PAY ATTENTION TO A CHILD'S EMOTIONS

1. Ross Campbell, *Relational Parenting* (Chicago: Moody Press, 2000), 42–43.
2. Ibid., 41–59, adapted.
3. John Gottman, and Joan Declaire, *The Heart of Parenting* (New York: Simon & Schuster, 1997), 50–51, adapted.
4. Ibid., 52, adapted.
5. Ibid., 73–74, adapted.
6. Mary Sheedy Kurcinka, *Kids, Parents, and Power Struggles*

(New York: HarperCollins, 2000), 4, adapted.
7. Archibald Hart, *Stress and Your Child* (Dallas: Word, Inc., 1992), 224.
8. David Ferguson et al., *Parenting with Intimacy* (Colorado Springs: Victor Books, 1995), 82–83.
9. Kurcinka, *Kids, Parents,* 13–14, adapted.

SECRET 10
GREAT PARENTS AVOID THESE TEN STEPS TO DISASTER

1. Foster Cline and Jim Fay, *Parenting With Love and Logic* (Colorado Springs: NavPress, 1990), 83, adapted.
2. Nancy Samalin, *Loving Your Child Is Not Enough* (New York: Penguin Books, 1998), 14, adapted.
3. Ibid.
4. Ray Guarendi, *Back to the Family* (New York: Villard Books, 1990), 135–36.
5. Denis Donovan and Deborah McIntyre, *What Did I Just Say?* (New York: Henry Holt, 1999), 7–8, adapted.
6. Robert J. MacKenzie, *Setting Limits* (Rocklin, CA: Prima Publishing, 1998), 42–55, 74–85, adapted.
7. John Gray, *Children Are From Heaven* (New York: HarperCollins, 1999), 244–45, adapted.
8. Becky A. Bailey, *Easy to Love, Difficult to Discipline* (New York: William Morrow & Co., 2000) 15–16, adapted.

SECRET 11
GREAT PARENTS LEARN TO BE LIMIT-SETTERS

1. Henry Cloud and John Townsend, *Boundaries with Kids* (Grand Rapids: Zondervan, 1999), 52.
2. Ibid., 52.
3. Ibid., adapted.
4. Wes Haystead, *The 3000 Year-Old Guide to Parenting* (Ventura, CA: Regal Books, 1991), 104–6.
5. Cloud and Townsend, *Boundaries with Kids,* 19–21, adapted.
6. Ibid., 40.
7. Foster Cline and Jim Fay, *Parenting with Love and Logic* (Colorado Springs: NavPress, 1990), 61, adapted.
8. Robert J. MacKenzie, *Setting Limits* (Rocklin, CA: Prima Publishing, 1998), 2–11, adapted.
9. Cloud and Townsend, *Boundaries with Kids,* 110–11.
10. Ibid., 104–5.
11. MacKenzie, *Setting Limits,* 13, adapted.
12. Cline and Fay, *Parenting with Love and Logic,* 62.
13. Ibid., 67, adapted.
14. Ron Taffel, *Parenting by Heart* (New York: Addison-Wesley Publishing, 1991), 172.
15. Cline and Fay, *Parenting with Love and Logic,* 92–93.
16. MacKenzie, *Setting Limits,* 73–190, adapted.
17. Ray Guarendi, *Back to the Family* (New York: Villard Books, 1990), 305, adapted.
18. Cloud and Townsend, *Boundaries with Kids,* 67, adapted.
19. John Gray, *Children Are From Heaven* (New York:

Harper Collins, 1998), 272–73, adapted.
20. Ibid., 273–74.
21. Randy Rolfe, *Letting Go* (Chicago: Contemporary Books, 1997), 133.

SECRET 12
GREAT PARENTS STAY FOCUSED ON THE FINAL GOAL

1. Rick Hicks and John Trent, *Seeking Solid Ground* (Colorado Springs: Focus on the Family), 60–61, adapted.
2. Ray Guarendi, *Back to the Family* (New York: Villard Books, 1990), 162–63.
3. Elizabeth Ellis, *Raising a Responsible Child* (Secaucus, NY: Citadel Press, 1996), 75–77, adapted.
4. Stormie Omartian, *The Power of a Praying Parent* (Eugene, OR: Harvest House, 1995), 13–14.
5. Ken Gire, *The Reflective Life* (Colorado Springs: Chariot Victor Publishing, 1998), 82–83.

About the Author

Dr. H. Norman Wright is a Gold Medallion winner and author of over seventy books, including the number one best-seller, *Always Daddy's Girl* (Regal Books). He is a licensed marriage, family, and child therapist, a grief-trauma therapist, and former professor at the Talbot School of Theology and Biola University where he directed their Graduate Department of Marriage, Family, and Child Counseling. He and his wife, Joyce, have been married for almost fifty years and have raised a son, now deceased, and a daughter. Norm and Joyce now live in Bakersfield, California.

Additional copies of *Be a Great Parent*
and other Life Journey titles are available
wherever good books are sold.

If you have enjoyed this book,
or if it has had an impact on your life,
we would like to hear from you.

Please contact us at:

Life Journey Books
Cook Communications Ministries, Dept. 201
4050 Lee Vance View
Colorado Springs, CO 80918

Or visit our Web site:
www.cookministries.com